Beyond Caregiving

A Caregiver's Guide on Coping with the Challenges of Disability, Aging, and Beyond

Romwell M. Sabeniano, MBA.HCM

authorHOUSE®

AuthorHouse™
1663 Liberty Drive
Bloomington, IN 47403
www.authorhouse.com
Phone: 833-262-8899

This book is a work of non-fiction. Unless otherwise noted, the author and the publisher make no explicit guarantees as to the accuracy of the information contained in this book and in some cases, names of people and places have been altered to protect their privacy.

Published by AuthorHouse 10/05/2020

ISBN: 978-1-6655-0122-4 (sc)
ISBN: 978-1-6655-0121-7 (e)

Library of Congress Control Number: 2020918496

Print information available on the last page.

This book is printed on acid-free paper.

Contents

Acknowledgement

I dedicate this book to my wife Cecilia, and to my daughter Ysabel for giving me the unconditional love, to my son Miguel Antonio for the profound memories, and inspiration, to my mom Modesta Rosario Sabeniano, my brother Joy Dennis and my sisters Myriam, Judith, and Carol, to my niece Ciara, my nephews Hamilton, Ennio, Nathan, and Seth for their support. I also would like to thank my editor, and my research staff, who helped me put this book together. My special thanks to all the people I met on my journey in this lifetime, including the patients and residents, parents, and direct-care staff I worked with during my 14-year career as Case Manager-Social Worker at a non-profit organization in the Counties of Riverside and San Bernardino. My gratitude also goes to the residents and healthcare professionals of several hospitals, group homes and nursing homes who gave me guidance during my 5-year service as Social Services Director in the Counties of Los Angeles and the Inland Empire area. It is with profound honor to advocate for the hundreds of homeless patients, the medically fragile, the cognitively and mentally challenged individuals whom I learned so much from their sincere friendship.

And most of all, I would like to thank GOD for the gift of health, family, and love as He guided me through the different challenges in my life. Thank you all for the inspiration you shared, which enabled me to write and publish this book after more than 8 years of research and preparation.

Romwell Martinez Sabeniano, MBA.HCM
Author-Publisher

Preface

Why is this book important to read? Beyond Caregiving contains a plethora of information that the reader will find very useful in coping with the challenges of providing care. In a nutshell, the book is about the deeper understanding of the role of a caregiver, learning creative ways to secure much need resources and services, maneuvering through the complex health care system, and most of all learning to enjoy and see the positivity in everything we do despite what life may bring to our fruitful undertaking. The book cover is a metaphor illustration of life's wonderful journey to affirm that caregiving is without boundaries, and no limits if we only commit our heart, and our mind to it.

We will personally experience disability, aging, and death through a loved one, a friend, client, or someone we casually meet during our lifetime. We or someone we know will experience injury, a personal illness, or unexplained debilitating disability inherent in our genes, possibly caused either by natural occurrence gifted to us from our family heritage, aging, or by an accident.

Let us imagine for a moment, a family member or a friend was born with a developmental disability or acquire some form of physical or cognitive challenges that make him dependent on you or others for the rest of his life? The unexpected event suddenly shifts from bad to worse as we confront it face-on, but we are left unprepared for its impact, either long or short term. Imagine if you or someone you know will undergo this painful and stressful experience, helpless, not knowing what to do, how to deal with the illness, and nobody to turn to for help. More often, caregivers do not know how to go about it as they feel alone and helpless, without financial resources or support to go through the complicated healthcare delivery system.

As an educator and advocate for the disabled and the developmentally challenged for 14 years; and as a Social Services Director at several skilled nursing facilities for 5-years, I witnessed most of the challenges that caregivers' and their families face up in dealing with the task. My goal in writing this book is to help alleviate caregiver stress in navigating through the difficult emotional, psychological, and financial challenges of caregiving. The book shall serve as a caregiver's guide in maneuvering through the complex healthcare delivery system and present creative ideas in procuring much-needed support from private entities, state and federally funded programs, and services available in the community.

The book also illustrates steps, and possible solutions in the appeals process that a caregiver may apply in the event of an unjust or unfair denial of rights of a developmentally challenged adult or a child. The goal is to mitigate the out-of-pocket costs of an already financially burdened population. The information presented in this book is locally available in the community for free or mostly at a low cost. However, people are not aware of them unless someone shows them the way or through personal experience at some point and time.

Beyond Caregiving likewise presents real-life cases and situations experienced by actual patients that benefitted from the author's services during his career as a social worker-case manager. However, the names of persons cited were altered to protect their information's privacy. The knowledge and information presented are based on successfully resolved cases and theories that may serve as a sampler or as an alternative solution to common situations in certain institutions, whether medical, social, or financial. Let it be a caveat that there are no guarantees as to the outcome in the cases cited are unique, and that patient situations may vary.

In reading the book, the reader will understand why it is difficult to provide care to different people, particularly patients with unique developmental challenges. The reader will also discover the correlation between aggressive behavior and medical disability, which explains why people act the way they do, sometimes even without reason. As caregivers, we need to understand why individuals act out or have behavior issues, especially those with cognitive, and functional challenges who cannot express their medical issues and pains. For purposes of discussion, let us say for instance, those who are profoundly developmentally disabled suffering from Aphasia (caused by brain damage) who "act out" without any precedence nor antecedent. Sometimes, our patient does not even have any known underlying condition that leads to a sudden outburst of emotion or aggression which we find challenging as caregivers. Part of the objective here is to be able learn the complexities of caregiving and present possible solutions to address them.

After writing three other books: "An Easy Guide on How to Establish Your First Residential Care Facility", "Caregiving: How to Start a Business of Providing Personalized In-Home Care Service" and Como Iniciar Una Pequenas y Medianas Empressas de Prestacion Personalizada En Servicio de Assistencia Domiciliaria (a Spanish translation of Caregiving:); I realized that there is more information that I needed to share besides the ones I already wrote in my previous books.

During my career as a Director for Social Services in a skilled nursing facility, I was a part of a team responsible in analyzing client's challenges and needs, psychological, medical, physical, and financial issues. Based on the information learned, I was responsible for assisting hundreds of patients, and their loved ones thrive and transition back in the community to live their normal lives or at least close to how it was before their confinement. I was fortunate to experience and understand the difficult challenges that my clients and their families face in dealing with the continuum of care, the lack of availability of community resources, and the defective post-hospitalization services. So, I hope that by writing this book, I could help others deal with their challenges as a caregiver and the receiver of care.

Introduction

Beyond Caregiving is about learning to define our roles and responsibilities as caregivers and a deeper understanding of why we provide care.

Almost on a daily basis, we face the daunting task of sharing unconditional love and care to our spouse, significant other, a parent, sibling, or a client. In this book, we will learn to value the importance of family and relationships; profound respect for life, health and most of all acknowledge the role of a higher being we respect and honor as GOD who has the power to comfort us beyond our realm. We will also learn to explore alternative choices in the healthcare delivery system and understand outcome of other approaches applied by patients before us to help resolve certain health issues or medical problem whether through medication, synthesized drugs, natural herbs, therapies, and other forms of alternative approach. There is no silver bullet nor a singular solution to all the caregiving issues out there, but the book will help us open our minds to alternative solutions other than what we already applied in our life, hoping it would mitigate the challenges that confronts us specially when we cannot reach a comforting resolution.

Beyond Caregiving does not attempt to encourage nor advocate for the use of unorthodox and unconventional treatment other than those recommended by the individual patients' physicians and other health care professionals. Every approach is unique and different in itself. The use of creative ideas are tempting, and are always welcome especially in desperate situations where one is left without much choices. The author merely cites cases he personally encountered that yielded positive results despite the presence of certain unknown calculated risks. Let it be clear however, that due to the uniqueness of the cases cited, the outcome is sometimes irrelevant to the particular individual's defined challenges. One may define it as divine intervention as others may see it as unexplained. Since the author is not a licensed professional on the subjects discussed in this book, the resolutions offered are mere representations of the uniquely undefined approaches that one may use as alternative options as results may vary depending on a given particular situation. There is no form of misrepresentation of false hope nor misleading information here, but merely presenting real cases that yielded encouraging outcomes that might be or may not be useful to the personal situation of the reader.

And now, let us sit back, relax and enjoy our journey as we read and understand the challenges Beyond Caregiving.

Chapter 1

The Caregiver

A caregiver is a person, a professional, non-professional, or a relative who provides direct care or some form of temporary assistance such as physical, emotional, psycho-social, financial, medical, and other form of support to a recipient of care temporarily while the other person is unable to manage to do things independently.

For discussion purposes, we will limit our definition of a caregiver as a person that provides care to others and or to self. The subject may apply to both the server and the recipient in the same instance. A caregiver can be someone who delivers professional assistance such as a nurse, a hired staff from an independent agency, or a family member. The fundamental goal is helping someone with limited capacities that require assistance in bathing, eating, hygiene, ambulation, and toileting. A caregiver is an exceptional person who takes the time, energy, and genuine sympathy to stop, listen, and care.

In our lifetime, regardless of our status in society, wealth, and belief, someday, we will eventually get sick or acquire an illness that could render us incapable of providing care to ourselves or providing aid to others for at least a certain limited time. Even machines wear down and break within its warranted time. A disability is not an anathema or a simple curse that we can ignore or set aside in our lifetime. Getting sick is nature's way of telling us that no matter how fit and healthy we are, we need to slow down and listen to our bodies as we are merely humans. Like machines, we have physical limitations. Despite the limitless resources, intelligence, and technological advancement of our world, we can not prevent illness, disease, or injury. Somehow, that unexpected and unexplainable illness will befall us at a moment we least expect it.

However, there are several ways to deal with it whenever it comes. The most practical approach is to be humble and acknowledge the healing presence of a higher power beyond our realm, whom we recognize as our ultimate personal caregiver and healer...GOD. A caregiver comforts our body while He lifts our spirit and heals our soul. We need to learn how to cope with what life teaches us in God's terms, one day at a time. To prepare ourselves with the challenge, we must first appreciate that caregivers are limited essentials, significantly when we are all impacted by the aging generation before us.

A Generation In Crisis

Based on the July 2016 census, the growing number of aging population within the United States will be approximately 74 million "baby boomers" (born between 1946-1964), 82 million "generation X" (born between 1965-1980), 71 million "generation Y or millennials" (born between 1981-1996), and 74 million "Gen Z" (the newest generation, born between 1995-2015). Our realization of the contrast in the age gap among the generations is crucial to our understanding of caregiving's impact on the current aging population. The four population groups and other succeeding generations thereafter, are expected to complement and support each other's growth and services. The "baby boomers" and "generation X" are already reaching their ages between the mid 60's and early 80's, but they have outgrown in disproportionate numbers that the succeeding generations that are expected to provide support are unable to prepare for the prior aging generation's care and service needs.

As a new wave of generations approach, it seems that there is a significant disparity among the group. It poses a grave threat in meeting the much-needed support and resources allocated for each other. Besides the inadequacies in resources, there is a huge incongruity caused by the vast age gap among the ages, interests, and family orientation. By 2025, there will be more than 90 million Americans who will turn 65 years old. The massive group of aging Americans (not to mention the foreign nationals migrating into the US) will at least once or a couple of times in a year, fall ill, or become bedridden. They will require temporary assistance, whether physically getting in and out of bed, taking medications, going to therapy sessions, doing errands, buying medicines and groceries, and other simple yet very challenging tasks, particularly those with physical and cognitive limitations. Frequently, a simple chore such as self-care or mobility can be downright tricky or even impossible, particularly for a person who lives alone with a debilitating illness. In short, besides the growth data provided, there will be many individuals who will be sick or aging, yet there are only a few people who can provide needed care and support. Hence, without a doubt, the task of caregiving will be overwhelming within the next few decades.

Caregiving is a universal combination of love, patience, sympathy, understanding, and care. Life can be very unpredictable most of the time. In the year 2020, a global pandemic known as the Coronavirus (Covid19), has caused a significant change in our lifestyle and how we perceive life. We learned the value of cleanliness and social distancing without compromising our perception of other's cultures, beliefs, and rights. We are now entering this new world we now know as the new normal. We never expected that this disease could change the whole planet, which proves, yet again, that anything can happen anytime when we least expect it. With this new world comes new changes in our culture, practices, and especially how we provide care to ourselves and others.

Nobody is exempt from the possibility of an illness or injury at any time. A simple slip or fall during a leisurely walk in the park or a menial chore at home could lead to an unpleasant surprise. An accident can happen anytime, and it is not a matter of if, but rather when. A small headache resulting from a minor slip and fall may turn into a significant cranial surgery that could lead to a temporary disability or permanent paralysis. There are also those cases of individuals who are born with physical and developmental challenges, which causes are still unknown to this day. Others may be coming home from a hospital or a place where they were exposed to an unknown bacteria or virus, forcing them to nurse an undiagnosed illness that could cause complex medical care. There will be people who live a perfectly normal life for a day then, with a twist of fate in one second, their life changes. They have to face the realization that a simple task of just getting out of bed, brushing teeth, or eating has now turned into a major obstacle that they have to go through for days, weeks, months, years, or even worse, a lifetime. Who else can they turn to for help to make it through the day is a fair question that can only be answered with... a caregiver.

The Caregiver's Roles and Responsibilities

Each caregiver has a different set of roles and responsibilities that are highly dependent on the recipient's specific needs. Caregivers are the voice, the advocate, the protector, the overseer, whom the recipient of trust look up to, someone who would give them the right treatment with dignity and respect.

First and foremost, a caregiver must respect other people's opinions, cultures, likes, and sense of character and individuality. We all have our thoughts and beliefs that we live by, but they may not always be right and proper. As a caregiver, we need to open our minds and learn from others. In the realm of caregiving, we as caregivers have the responsibility of respecting other people's wishes and requests as long as they are within reason, legal, and ethical. The nature and outcome of providing care are relatively dependent on how we, as caregivers, can cope with our understanding of diversity, ethnicity, mental health, and religion, among others, to provide effective care and make appropriate health care decisions.

The caregiver's past experiences and understanding of the varying degrees of care play a significant role in making healthcare decisions. There are tons of things in this life that we, human caregivers, do not know, however we will eventually learn as we go along with the challenges and the experiences. Prior knowledge and experience could be an essential tool in a caregiver's daily battle with the tasks required to reduce the considerable risk involved. Learning through our personal experience, reading books on similar subjects, including the regulations and laws, asking health care professionals, and consulting with others who share similar situations or challenges are the caregiver's endless but practical tasks.

To be effective caregivers, we must be creative in navigating through the confusing healthcare system. We must learn to integrate the information that we acquire from the patient, physician, health care professionals, relatives, and other sources such as books, Internet, or other means to be able to make informed decisions.

Care recipients and caregivers face challenges and personal issues such as language barriers, literacy, privacy, finance, cultural differences, pain tolerance, and other unexplained reasons. As caregivers, we should be able to process and learn to integrate our experience with the circumstances of our recipients for us to be able to meet the challenges that come with our role.

Who else can advocate for your loved one except themselves and you?

Have you ever experienced talking to someone in the morning, then the following day, find out that he is in a coma, fighting for his life in the hospital just merely because he choked on his food during his dinner? If you think that will never happen to you, think again.

Let me tell you a true story about a client named Shawn, 36 years old, non-ambulatory, non-verbal, diagnosed with mild mental retardation, cerebral palsy, and profound spastic quadriplegia, seizure disorder, and has a history of choking. One day, I received a call from a hospital stating that my client is in a coma and might not make it the next morning. Upon receiving the news, I learned that he has no chance of recovery, and that his family decided to pull the plug on his life-sustaining equipment; I was shocked. My immediate response was to rush to the hospital and identified myself as the client's social worker at the nurse's station. I came in just a few seconds to bid my farewell to Shawn before catching his last breath. I have known Shawn for more than five years as a client and as a friend, where I learned a lot from him as his case manager advocating for his developmental challenges.

I remember another interesting consumer named Martin, 41 years old, who was born with a diagnosis of profound mental retardation, non-verbal and non-ambulatory. Martin is confined to the hospital for choking on his food. When I saw Martin in the emergency wing, I noticed that he was in a room with a group of patients with the least cognitive functioning abilities and only one supervising nurse. He is confined in a room located at the hospital building's rear wing, where one could hardly hear or notice even if he yells. When I interviewed the staff caregiver, she told me that Martin's meal has the consistency of a solid mass instead of pureed close to the consistency of a liquid diet. A CNA-caregiver was about to give him his salad bowl and a turkey in a cube-shaped sandwich with milk on the side. I reminded the caregiver that the prescribed meal is pureed. If uncorrected, Martin would regurgitate and choke on his meal. There was a miscommunication between the hospital and the group home where he lives. A minor mistake in information on Martin's meal requirement could have caused a tragic error if left uncorrected.

The lesson to be learned here is that we caregivers should know our clients appropriately based on what was prescribed by their physician, what they like, why they are in our care. By reading their medical records and nurses' notes, observing their abilities, and by opening our minds we can learn more about our clients. We can predict and hopefully prevent injuries or accidents while they are in our care through this practice. No matter how busy we are, as caregivers, we must seriously take the time to get to know more about our care-recipient, especially those who are developmentally delayed and physically challenged.

The Caregiver's Challenges

The most common responsibility of a caregiver is to assist the recipient of care in almost everything that the person is unable to do, primarily with activities of daily living like walking, eating, dressing, medicine, bathing, and a lot of other undefined tasks. Sometimes even simple tasks such as scratching an itch, putting on a gown or slippers, and putting on a pair of reading glasses, makeup, or underwear.

But the challenge is merely starting. We must honor people's mindset that reflects their personal preference and opinion. We must learn to support them by understanding their frustration due to their inability to do the things they are used to before their injury. People develop a form of resistive behavior due to guilt and frustration to cope with their medical issues. This behavior frequently may lead to other medical problems such as early signs of aging, chronic illness, disease, memory loss, and even dementia.

Moreover, we must not forget that receivers of care can develop medical and nursing issues that would elevate the caregiver's responsibilities to a different level. Such, an example, may include other additional duties like managing catheters, skin integrity care around a central pic line, gastrostomy tube feedings, and ventilators. These additional responsibilities may virtually lead caregivers to their breaking point.

In my experience, I observed that caregivers' most common challenges are lack of knowledge and experience, lack of rest and resources, and communication.

Knowledge and experience

It is common for family caregivers to develop the feeling of confusion and unpreparedness in handling their overwhelming responsibility. The lack of adequate knowledge to deliver quality care is partially attributed to physicians, nurses, and other therapists' deficient guidance. The inadequacy of knowledge and skills as caregivers are also observed due to the absence of familiarity with the type of care required. As a result, family caregivers end up overwhelmed with stress and frustration. Eventually, they tend to ignore their responsibilities outside of caregiving, such as their own families, jobs, and health, compromising their well-being.

The caregiver's lack of experience, knowledge, and skills necessary to maintain their roles and responsibilities could lead to an elevated risk not only to the recipients of care but also to themselves.

Lack of rest and resources

Caregivers' stress may cause inadequate rest and exercise, which may lead to illness. Also, due to the burdensome task focused on caring for others, caregivers are more likely to ignore their personal needs. With all the confusing and stressful demands of providing care, sometimes people tend to ignore their overall health as caregivers compromising their ability to continue as caregivers.

No matter how hectic our daily schedule is, we as caregivers need to balance our jobs, activities, and family responsibilities. Moreover, we need to have time for our recreation to decompress from the daily grind. If we do not do that, we will end up breaking-down emotionally, physically, and mentally.

When we get sick, our financial situation becomes drastically affected, further aggravating our situation. According to a leading study, most caregivers who provide aid to family members and friends have regular jobs of their own. When they are over-burdened with providing care, most of the time, they bring the stress at home and at work where they sometimes unload.

Stress and anxiety often cause a negative impact, leading to family-and-work-related problems. Families argue and sometimes become aggressive and violent. As a worker, a caregiver becomes temperamental. She might be late or absent at work, disrupting the workflow and production. The conflicts might lead to illness, job loss, or worse, death.

Some would be lucky if their work environment offers relief to decompress from the stress. But others who are not fortunate enough end up in a worse situation than before they came to work. Family caregivers with sufficient funds have less of a challenge, but those who lack available personal financial resources could lead a caregiver to another level of stress as daily expenses mount and pile up until they eventually break down.

Constant stress to a caregiver on top of financial issues could lead to depression. The level of stress is higher when the recipient of care requires a higher level of personalized services, particularly for the elderly and those with mental health issues. Most caregivers unprepared for their roles as providers of care can be attributed to lack of experience and lack of knowledge of the issues involved. Therefore they experience a deeper and more confusing level of stress.

Caregivers will have a tremendous challenge of navigating through the discharge process from hospital to home or a nursing facility. They must be supplied with adequate resources, including a specific plan of care that is written out in detail, indicating the type of care needed and a referral list of health care professionals involved in the continuum of care to minimize the impact of risk to the patient they serve. There must be a care planning process discussed in detail. It is essential to help ease the transition and promote safety and support for caregivers.

Care recipients' intellectual functioning, cognitive skills, and emotional status are predictable signs that can fairly gauge the caregiver's challenges. The caregiver's stress in response to the problems that evolved from the provision of care is often manifested in feelings of loneliness, isolation, fearfulness, and being easily irritable. The demands of caregiving limit their space and personal time. Behaviors such as screaming, yelling, swearing, and threatening are tell tale signs of increased caregiver stress and depression leading to somatic component, such as anorexia, injuries, infection, fatigue, exhaustion, and insomnia. Any fluctuation in sleep patterns could lead to depression and exacerbate symptoms of chronic illnesses. Stress can be adversely harmful to both the caregiver and the care recipient.

Another concern is that, with the demanding work of caregiving, caregivers are at risk of engaging in possible harmful behaviors toward their care recipients, especially those with developmental disabilities. A caregiver who is confronted with stressful situations, especially those close to their breaking point, is more likely to harm, neglect, or abuse their care recipients, especially those related to them. Caregivers who are at risk of depression while providing care for individuals who require higher and more complex care due to their disabilities tend to engage in abusing, screaming, yelling, threatening, or using physical force when dealing with their frustrations.

The Art of Communication

Communication or the lack thereof can transform a simple chore to total confusion or chaos. Henceforth, it is significant to clarify and, if possible, translate verbally through repetition, use of written material, sign language, body gestures, or other possible ways of communicating that are easy to understand. There are also other means of communication that are unexplainable that can only be bridged solely through a bonding relationship between the caregiver and the recipient of care. It can be a form of touch, a stare, a look, a smile, or even a wink that only the caregiver and the recipient understand as a result of bonding and genuine love.

Proper communication is a critical element in every interaction. It may become a challenge when one is unable to understand what the other party is trying to convey. Communication is often an issue of cultural or internal misunderstanding instead of a mere verbal defect in interpreting a given meaning. When communication is lost somewhere in translation such as missing the actual issue, communication becomes very stressful to all of the parties involved, like the caregiver, care recipients, health care professionals, and the families. Since we will be dealing mostly with issues of care recipients, including the developmentally challenged, the subject of communication is crucial in avoiding misunderstandings and further complications. Please keep it simple, clear, and loud enough to hear what is was being pronounced. If possible, repeat the words to confirm the task requested.

Besides verbal communication, a caregiver's role is to listen carefully and attentively to make the task simple and effective. Hearing with your ears is good, but it only becomes effective when listening with your eyes and your gut feelings. If you look carefully at the care recipient, there are telltale signs you can keenly observe and follow through. A caregiver's role can sometimes be overwhelming, particularly when the day-to-day route of caregiving gets misaligned and becomes out of focus. As a caregiver, you must learn to slow down once in a while to reflect on your role and its impact on people around you. It is very important to figure out if we are connected well emotionally and psychologically with our loved ones and our care recipients. It is as simple as improving our listening skills. Most of the time, we go beyond listening, using that extra sense known as common sense.

Stop, Look and Listen Carefully

As a caregiver, we may have a long to-do-list that is often endless, but what matters most is the time well spent to sit down and listen to our recipient of care. Spend a brief moment and truly commit yourself to listen to an interaction. Worry less about other tasks if they remain unfinished. A conversation time focused on the unspoken signs or words from a care-recipient, or a family member is worth a thousandfold. Listen with your eyes and look for visual and non-verbal cues from someone with cognitive and verbal challenges. Maintaining eye contact throughout your conversation and focusing on other body languages, can help you not only hear what's being said, but also hear those loud signs that often speak through silent words.

Encourage the patient to speak on their terms.

When helping someone deal with their unspoken soft issues, please encourage them to communicate their concerns and feelings on their phase and terms. It helps display respect and gentleness when you encourage them to take the time and wait and listen. Be a pro-active listener and allow them to express their feelings. One of the best forms of emotional support you can provide is to be there and simply listen. Although you may be unable to fix the problem, listening can help the person feel heard and validated. Emotions are likely to change over time and can vary depending on their level of severity.

Asking how the person feels may result in different reactions depending on things like general mood, the quality of sleep they had the night before, and how high and low their tolerance for pain is at the time of the interaction. Listening to how the patient describes her current feelings will enable you to predict how far the conversation may take.

Communication Tips:

(a). Encourage the patient to tell you more about his or her feelings. Ask open-ended follow-up questions to the things they say and avoid issues that result in a short yes/no answer. Share your thoughts and ideas to get the conversation started. Don't be discouraged if the person in your care isn't as enthusiastic to talk as you are.

Pay attention to nonverbal communication, such as body language and lack of eye contact, for clues about how the person may be feeling. In time, you will become familiar with the particular non-verbal cues that the person may display. Sharing your fears and emotions can help break the ice if the person seems reluctant to tell you what they are feeling. You may be surprised at their reactions to what you can personally share.

(b). Avoid phrases that tend to shut the conversation down or seem dismissive to what the person is feeling. For example, phrases like "Don't worry about that," "You'll be just fine," or "What do the doctors know anyway?" can make someone feel as if their concerns aren't relevant to you. Listen more and talk less. Give the person a chance to speak without interruption.

(c). Repeat back what the person has said to make sure that you understand. Ask for clarification if you are not sure what they mean. Offer assurance that you will try to help with the person's physical, emotional, and spiritual needs. Let the person know how you plan on helping resolve their issues.

(d). Help the person focus on what he or she is still able to do. Help them find ways around tasks that they find challenging. Remain positive, and look for small ways to make tasks enjoyable. Make eye contact when you are talking. Smile and engage in active listening to show you are interested in what they have to say.

(e). Avoid deep conversations when you are rushed for time. Set aside time to discuss important issues or topics that the person is interested in discussing. Express yourself physically and verbally like a touch on the hand, stroking the hair, or a kiss on the cheek can make a difference. A gentle touch can often be reassuring. Please encourage them to express themselves through writing or hand movements and other body languages. When people who are ill have trouble speaking, they may understand far more than they can say.

(f). Reach out for help if you need assistance with your feelings. Support can come from another family member, a social worker, nurse, doctor, chaplain, or spiritual advisor. Sometimes an outside perspective can be helpful between you and the other person. Being a compassionate listener is most important, particularly when you pass on essential information to others. Providing the person in your care with information about their condition can help ease uncertainty and fear of the unknown. Some people will want to know everything all at once, while others will want the information to come in stages.

In my experience as a case manager for a licensed facility, healthcare professionals were puzzled about my client Jonathan, an adult, cognitively challenged and unable to clearly express his thoughts. On a typical day, Jonathan enjoys brief walks in the garden with a staff. However, on this particular fine day, Jonathan refused to do his walk. He preferred to lay in bed. He kept poking his left ear and showed increased signs of agitation, which is promptly perceived as assaultive aggression. The nurse's typical response was to give him psychotropic medications. A few moments later, Jonathan continued his non-compliant behavior as he kept poking and digging his ears. A nurse was called in and requested to do an ear exam using an Otoscope and to check Jonathan's temperature. The ear exam revealed a minor infection of the ear canal, so Jonathan was taken to the hospital in-patient care unit. Upon his return, he remained quiet and compliant to all requests, and he participated in all activities. In conclusion, most of the time, behavior can not always be addressed with psychotropic medication but taking the time to listen to the patient's unspoken words.

Remind yourself as to how others might perceive you. Keep your body language in check as there are certain gestures and movements that may be misunderstood as barriers to communication due to the messages they convey. For example, crossed arms may be perceived as stubborn or defensive, while putting your hands on your hips may be interpreted as aggressive or confrontational. Sometimes even professional caregivers need to step back and remember the importance of listening and knowing that patients or family members are also present.

Be A Pro-Active Listener

Always ask questions to show compassion and care. Look for signs of concerns, hoarding, lack of appetite or lack of interest, depressions, signs of possible neglect, or abuse. Perhaps your loved one is telling you something you already know. Maybe you've heard this story or had this discussion multiple times before. While these types of talks may be easy to dismiss, reframing each conversation could be an opportunity to deepen your bond with your aging loved one or offers a different and valuable point of view. Even when you have tons of things to do, do not rush the patient into an answer; instead, hold the conversation for a later day or time. Just be sure to discuss it again when you have the time.

Working on your communication, listening, and open-mindedness can be vital in building the most positive patient-caregiver relationships. The time is always right. Each day offers a new opportunity to become a better listener and a better caregiver in the process.

Caregiver's Assessment

Given the enormous responsibility to provide the proper care, solid teamwork must be established between the healthcare professionals and the caregiver before the care-receiver's endorsement. Therefore, the healthcare staff and caregiver must assess whether there will be sufficient provision of resources and care coordination. The caregiver must carefully assess whether she is ready to take on the responsibility and maintain the balance between her role as a caregiver to the patient and her family.

The caregiver's assessment of the task required is critical, including identifying possible risk factors for abuse and neglect to understand the role entirely.

Caregiver's Resources

Linking caregivers to any available community resources is important because caregivers are often unaware that support services are available. The caregiver must be provided with accessible, much-needed resources from delivering care services to securing financial assistance and placements in government-funded facilities and hospitalization expenses. The caregiver will appreciate resources helpful in dealing with the confusing bureaucracy of obtaining goods and services through Medicaid, Medicare. Veterans Benefits, etc... The world-wide-web, aka Internet, is a very important resource tool that anyone can use nowadays to help them clarify matters from "How to Videos" on Youtube to What is it?, Google, Yahoo and hundreds of search engines. One can find everything there is to know and to understand millions of processed information and services available in the community that is available within the palms of their hands. A recent study of caregivers for people with Alzheimer's disease found that 75 percent had unmet needs. Yet, only 9 percent had used respite services, and only 11 percent had participated in support groups. It simply indicates that people rarely use free or inexpensive community resources because they refuse to or do not know it exists.

Caregiver's Interventions

In this technically advanced day and age, we expect people to be more aware of the latest issues affecting themselves, those with low cognitive function, limited skill potential, and those born with developmental disabilities. Interventions to improve knowledge and experience supported with patient compatibility with the caregiver is a-must in enhancing caregiver skills and minimizing stress and frustration. Interventions should consider potential confounding risk variables such as low-income family relationships, cultural variation, caregiver health status, stage of the disease, and hours of care. They are essential in effectively managing caregiver stressor symptoms. To mitigate and control caregiver breakdown, they must also have continuous training and therapy. Furthermore, there must be a focus on variations or adaptations in minimizing caregiver stress related to ethnic, racial, cultural, or socio-economic diversity.

Interventions will improve patient outcomes that are particularly essential to building a high-quality system of continuing care. Caregivers who face conflicts in competing demands related to caring for their children, spouse, or parent and maintaining their work roles are significantly affected by the vulnerable demands of provision of care. Caregivers need external support outside of their circle because it aids in the reduction of the frequencies of patient or caregiver hospital admissions, lessen interruptions in treatment cycles, shortens work loss period, and attain better patient-caregiver mental health. Quality of care and patient safety will dramatically improve once they meet these needs.

The caregiver must engage in activities that promote their health and well-being. Without a doubt, stress may lead to depression, which affects the caregiver's behavior and decision-making skills. These factors have a significant negative impact on the caregiver and care-recipient relationship.

Finally, interventions must include unifying healthcare professionals, caregivers, and family as partners in the entire care planning process.

The Caregiver's Prayer

In times when I am overwhelmed by exhaustion and frustration in my work, I read this Serenity Prayer written by the American theologian, *Reinhold Niebuhr.* It goes like this… *"GOD, grant me the serenity to accept the things I cannot change; the courage to change the things I can; and the wisdom to know the difference."*

Believe.

Faith and fate are two different words, and yet they share the same purpose in our life. Both terms may be complimentary and yet contradictory to each other, just like the iconic question: "Which came first, the chicken or the egg?" In a capsule, faith is a feeling, conviction, or belief that something is true or real, assent that is not contingent upon reason or justification. In contrast, fate is the presumed cause, force, principle, or divine will that predetermines events.

Faith and fate can be connected to our understanding of destiny. Depending on who you ask, the end may or may not justify the means or vice versa. In our popular western world view of destiny, we as individuals control our lives, and everything that happens to us is a result of our own choice. On the other hand, the popular eastern view is that everything that happens to us is not under our control. We are nothing but participants in a preordained plan. However, neither of these views is entirely correct. According to the science of Spirituality, in the present time, 65% of our lives are ruled by destiny and 35% by willful action. But we can overcome the 65% of our destiny part by using the 35% of our deliberate action to undertake the correct spiritual practice. As per spiritual science, destiny refers to matters we have no control over life situations. A Willful Act is that portion of our life which we do have control over.

In short, we need to do our part in bringing resolution to our issues by doing what is physically, meta-physically, economically, or whatever is necessary to accomplish our end goal. We can control and explain things in our life, and there are those matters that we cannot understand and cannot possibly control. In such cases, we must let them evolve on their own and leave our faith to control their fate.

Therefore, as caregivers, we need to have faith that we can handle and surpass our challenges. We have to do something about those within our control, like preparing ourselves for the situation, equipping ourselves with the much-needed knowledge and experience, and continuously learning to provide better assistance.

Once we have done everything on our part, it is time to let fate do its job.

Chapter 2

The Care Recipient

Who Is The Care Recipient?

In Caregiving in the U.S. 2015, the National Alliance for Caregiving (NAC) & AARP Public Policy Institute define the care recipient as the one who receives care. A care recipient is a person with a medical condition or an individual who necessitates support with daily living and day-to-day activities. The person may need a caregiver (a doctor, a nurse, a friend, a family member, etc.) who can provide support, assistance, treatment, comfort, and the like.

The care recipient's needs may vary from daily routine activities, medical and healthcare management, and personal treatment. Such requirements highly depend on the care recipient's situation and condition. A care recipient with dementia will require a different type of support compared to a care recipient with heart disease. Some cases depend on the age of the care recipient. Other factors to consider are the care recipient's gender, experiences, attitudes, and preferences.

Relationship To The Caregiver

It is essential for a care recipient to have a good relationship with her caregiver to achieve an efficient and successful way of providing care. It is beneficial for both parties because it can prevent miscommunication, risks, and conflicts. Having a bad relationship can also cause unnecessary added stress to both the care recipient and the caregiver, defeating Caregiving's ultimate purpose.

In establishing a good relationship, the care recipient's needs and wants must be clearly understood by the caregiver. The care recipient's goals and wishes must be discussed with the caregiver to assess the care recipient's essentials. Doing so also aids the caregiver to come up with an effective plan of care. There are care recipients who want to feel self-sufficient even though they need a caregiver. Others, would like to be well-informed regarding their condition, while there are some that do not appreciate receiving unsolicited pieces of advice. In general, people want to be a part of the decision on their healthcare.

If the care recipient's preferences were set aside, it might result in a clash between the two parties. Hence, to avoid such problems, the two parties need to settle what the caregiver can do for the care recipient, without compromising the care recipient's health, safety, and opinions.

The common factors to be considered are the following:

1. Degree of support
2. Decision-making
3. Competency
4. Appreciation

The amount of assistance that the care recipient needs from the caregiver should be clarified firsthand. The desired level of support varies from one care recipient to another. Sometimes a care recipient does not appreciate too much involvement from the caregiver. Some want to speak directly to the doctors or nurses instead of the caregiver. Being able to do so serves as an assurance for them that their voices are heard. Because in some cases, the caregiver might not be able to state in detail all the information about the care recipient's condition. Suppose the care recipient prefers to talk to the medical professional. In that case, the caregiver can add questions or even information that the care recipient missed out.

The care recipient should always be involved when it comes to decision-making because it is their health and safety that is at stake. When she feels that she is not involved in the decision-making process, she might refuse assistance and support, leading to further problems and conflicts. Therefore, the care recipient and the caregiver must develop plan of care that are agreeable to both of them, without sacrificing the care recipient's preferences and the caregiver's duties and responsibilities.

Belief in the caregiver's competency is vital because care recipients who do not trust their caregiver's abilities will not feel safe and secure. On the other hand, caregivers must also distinguish what the care recipients can and cannot do. The care recipient must be sure that her caregiver can take care of her, administer healthcare, and provide for her needs. Also, the caregiver should be aware of the capabilities of her care recipient to avoid incompatibility.

Appreciation is also essential because if one from the two parties feels unappreciated, this will lead to stress. Care recipients who do not feel appreciated might think that their caregivers had unrealistic expectations of them. Lack thereof might be the cause of aggravated health conditions. On the other hand, caregivers who feel taken for granted might be less efficient or even quit providing care.

Care recipients and caregivers must work together to achieve mutual understanding. Lack of coordination from both might end to drastic outcomes. Every care recipient is different and the same way that every caregiver is also diverse. Hence, both must establish a good relationship to accomplish beneficial consequences for both parties.

The Care Recipient Evaluation

Mike Good, the founder of Together in This, an organization aiming to help educate all caregivers by providing streamlined resources and easy to use tools, discussed three steps on adequately evaluating the care recipient. According to him, the three main factors to consider are:

> The care recipient's care needs
> The care recipient's state of affairs
> The care recipient's resources

Medication records, family member's health records, and family medical history are the documents that must be studied by the caregiver. These records can inform the caregiver about the medical and personal needs of the care recipient.

The care recipient's financial and legal situation should also be reviewed by the caregiver, particularly if he is a relative and may need to know its location in the event it is required. Pertinent documents comprise of medical and financial power of attorneys, living will, last will and testament, deeds on assets, and existing contracts.

The resources of the care recipient include family, loved ones, and friends. The caregiver must know whom to contact in times of need. The caregiver must also assess the level of commitment and support that the individual can provide for the care recipient to avoid problems and conflicts.

The Risk of Client Abuse

The risk of client abuse is prevalent among the aging population and individuals with developmental challenges, particularly those with profound mental retardation, non-verbal, non-ambulatory dementia, and cognitive-behavioral problems. They are at a higher risk of being abused and neglected as easy targets because most can not express their thoughts, needs, and wants. More so, they cannot speak the truth that they are being taken advantage of or abused. However, they can show some signs that anyone with the right mind and a clear conscience can figure out what is wrong. If only one would listen with their eyes and care to observe meticulously, one would discover what the care recipient wants to convey. An individual can look for signs of abuse or neglect through people's facial expressions, gestures, screaming, looks of fear, hate, and reflections of discontent. The care recipient's unspoken words can be expressed through their body language, mannerisms, gestures, or hand signals.

Signs To Look For When You Suspect
Possible Abuse or Neglect

When dealing with the aged and individuals with special needs, there are many things to consider. Neglect comes in different forms. It can be lack of proper nutrition and access to food, unmanaged pain, urinary incontinence, or falls are just a few signs among others. Caregiver neglect may occur because the care recipient can neither express her thoughts and feelings nor communicate them, making the caregiver unable to understand what is bothering her or incapable to deal with the particular problem that the care recipient is having such as pain, lack of nutrition, or even depression.

A common problem among family members as caregivers is that they neither have sufficient knowledge nor training on medication dispensing. As a result, medication dispensing error is very chronic. Most of these errors result in frequent hospitalization of their care recipients due to falls, behavior, or even death. It is also typical among the developmentally disabled population to have more than five medications at any given time. So, caregivers have difficulty keeping track of which medication is due and which one is not. When it happens, caregivers are unaware of the toxic effect of their errors such as vomiting, dehydration, diarrhea, and even hospitalization. Caregivers need to be educated accordingly to recognize the variable adverse effects of the drugs and its long-term consequence to their care recipients.

The most common sign of abuse or neglect in homes and licensed care facilities and yet rarely discussed, is medication error. A medication error may come in four different forms: wrong medication, wrong dosage, wrong time, and even wrong person.

Medication errors in nursing homes and other inpatient medical facilities are recognized as common medical problems. The nursing facility's frequency of medication errors must be kept below a standard or acceptable percentage of medication errors. If the medication error rate rises above that standard, the nursing facility will be required to create and enact a plan for correction. All facilities must maintain a nursing home medication error rate below 5% percent. While minor medicine errors are inevitable, nursing home residents must remain free of any severe medication errors. By definition, medication errors are mistakes that occur while preparing or administering medicine. The medication error occurs in a manner that contradicts the doctor's orders, the manufacturer's instructions, or the accepted professional standards.

In most nursing homes, medication is administered when a nurse or nursing staff member completes a "med pass." A "med pass" is the common term used to describe the process of dispensing medicine to nursing home patients as ordered. During a med pass, the nurse typically uses a cart while transitioning from resident to resident on a clearly-defined schedule. In most cases, a licensed nurse conducts the med pass. However, some states allow an unlicensed nursing staff member to administer the medication under the nurse's general supervision. The med pass typically requires 4 to 5 hours of the nurse's time during medication administration. Besides, it can take several more hours to organize the medications and complete any necessary documentation.

The most common medication errors in licensed facilities

The following is a list of commonly observed medical malpractice or medication errors that cause concern in licensed facilities which needs to be addressed:

(a). Ignoring medication orders. Some nursing home employees may ignore medication administration instructions on purpose. Examples include discontinuing elder medication, adding unordered medication, or changing the elder medication dosage.

(b). Poor elder medication management occurs when the nursing home fails to renew or maintain the specified medications, leaving the nursing home resident without the proper elder medication. This medication malpractice may occur through the poor organization, inadequate documentation, or defiant nursing staff actions.

(c). Medication borrowing. When the nursing home staff is busy during the med pass, they may be missing the proper elder medication due to poor organization. As a result, the person conducting the med pass may "borrow" a medication from one patient to give to another. This often occurs in conjunction with a failure to note or account for the borrowed medication, leading to more negligent medication errors and nursing home malpractice. Medication borrowing can also mask the diversion of medicines by causing confusion.

(d). Diversion of elder medications. When a nursing home staff member diverts medications, the staff member is stealing the medication for personal use. The nursing staff member may steal or divert a medication for actual use, or the nursing staff member may attempt to sell the stolen elder medications.

Neglect and Family Conflict

The caregiver's perception of the care situation is crucial in understanding the potential for harm. Caregivers bothered by other symptoms tend to assess patients' actual symptoms inaccurately. Neglect is more common when the caregiver is depressed or stressed. It interferes with the person's ability to make observations and identify needs or provide social stimulation for their ill family member. When caregivers themselves are burdened with stress, they might leave the care-receivers alone for long periods, ignore them, or fail to provide companionship or interaction. Research shows that care becomes inadequate when caregivers for patients with dementia reach their breaking point due to a high level of burden. The number of care demands and time per week, impaired sense of own identity, clinical fluctuations in the patient, and nocturnal deterioration in the patient predict the caregiver's breaking point.

When there is family conflict, there is less assistance to the patient resulting in an increase in negative patient behavior, aggravating further strain to the caregiver. Caregivers may also relinquish caregiving when they are unsuccessful in maintaining a relationship or when the care becomes problematic, particularly when the care recipient loses cognitive function. Conflicts can also occur with unfulfilled or mismatched aid. Negative interactions with kin include disparaging comments on caregiving, caregiver health status, and criticisms on care decisions.

Chapter 3

Coping with Disability

T o better understand our role as caregivers, we need to know the different types of disabilities that our receivers of care might have. First of all, we should ask ourselves this question...

What is a disability?

Disability is broadly defined as the consequence of an impairment that may be physical, cognitive, mental, sensory, emotional, developmental, or a combination of these. A disability may be acquired from birth or occur by accident or evolve from prior history during a person's lifetime. Disability is an umbrella definition that may encompass impairments, activity limitations, and participation restrictions. Impairments may include physical, sensory, and cognitive or developmental disabilities. Mental disorders (also known as psychiatric or psycho-social disability) and various types of chronic disease may also qualify as disabilities.

In different countries and organizations, disability is defined in a slightly different manner. Individual's disabilities are acquired differently from others as a disability may occur during a person's lifetime or may

be present from birth, and others occur by accident or illness. Disability can result from a physical condition, intrinsic to the individual, and that such illness reduces the person's quality of life.

The term disability is loosely used in just about any form of a person's physical limitations interchangeably confused with the term "handicap." As a blanket terminology, the definition of disability includes other words correlated to a person's challenges, whether physical, visual, mental, verbal, psycho-social, or developmental. Even as simple as a person being unable to see clearly is included in the broad definition of disability.

Handicap has been disparaged as a result of false folk etymology that is in close reference to begging. It is actually derived from an old game, *Hand-i-cap*, in which two players trade possessions, and a third, neutral person judges the difference of value between the possessions. Similarly, in golf, a handicap is termed to a player's challenges in completing the game. As early as the 19th century in Europe, the term "handicap" racing, horses carry different weights based on the umpire's estimation of what would make them run equally. In the early 20th century, the use of the term to describe a person with a disability, by extension from handicap racing, a person carrying a more substantial burden than usual, was typical. In the later years that follow, "handicap" replaced terms that are now considered insulting, such as "crippled" and has now evolved into a more civilized term such as physically-challenged, mentally-challenged, visually-impaired or developmentally-challenged for others born with the disability.

All disabled people are impaired, and all handicapped people are disabled. But a person can be impaired and not necessarily be disabled, and a person can be disabled without being handicapped.

How To Cope with Sudden Disability, Aging, and Death

To be able to cope with this challenge, we need to understand by looking back at the different types of disabilities. Illness and disability may come in many forms, as some are genetic or acquired from birth. In contrast, others are developed during the person's lifetime or caused by accident through the environment or nature taking its normal course.

A debilitating illness, whether genetically related or by accident, may come suddenly, or it could gradually develop over many years without the person knowing it. Some people may be born with the illness as others may acquire it from their environment or may be based on the lifestyle they chose, such as smoking, drinking, drug addiction, etc... Learning to cope with any illness is not always easy and might take a long time, especially when the illness comes with twists and surprises that we oftentimes are not prepared for.

Let us imagine that now you are on top of the world, happy, your life is going well, and you are very proud of all your accomplishments. You earned your degree and have a new, promising career, you are enjoying your friends and family's company. Suddenly, one day, this unfortunate event happens to you, and you receive the news from your physician that you are ill and can no longer do stuff that you usually enjoy. Or you got involved in an accident causing you to be no longer the same physically, mentally, or socially as you were yesterday. If not you, imagine your spouse, a child, relative, or a friend suddenly becomes ill, and you are left with the responsibility to care and provide support. Life, as you know, is no longer the same. All of a sudden, everything starts to fall apart, and you are confronted with all types of scary "what if" scenarios you can imagine. And suddenly, you become helpless, and you can no longer provide financial, physical, and emotional support for yourself and your family as your hopes and dreams are no longer there. That can be the most challenging time in your life, and it is normal that you feel naturally low. It may take a while for everything to sink in, but eventually, you need to convince yourself to snap out of it and visualize for yourself what will happen if you remain paralyzed and become complacent with what is in front of you.

However, after we have gone through the whole grieving process, now we have to decide at a turning point... to choose to remain in a "poor-me-and-blame-the-whole-world" attitude or be positive and try to look at the brighter side of life. We still have family, we're alive and the whole world is full of hope and opportunities. The choice to deal with the fear of the uncertainty in life is grave and daunting but it is a normal reaction to either freeze and run away. It purely depends on you and nobody else. Something must be done soon.

Here are a couple of things to cope with when such situation happens. Remember these as we go through the challenging journey towards change. These are only a few critical things that served as my pillars and strength during the darkest moments in my life. Moreover, I am proud to share them with you.

1. Think positive, and create a plan that you intend to commit to.
2. Don't be afraid to take baby steps.
3. Sleep and rest.
4. Believe and trust in God.
5. Read books that provide encouragement and support.
6. Surround yourself with good and honest people who provide support and friends who share the same thoughts and aspirations.
7. Always remember, never give up.
8. Nurture yourself.
9. Research on the illness and discover ways to deal with it. Enlighten your mind and learn to accept the new information that could change in your life.
10. Walk and feel one with nature.
11. Concentrate on the present. Do not dwell on the past or worry about the future.
12. Try hard to eliminate stress from your life.
13. You are the maker of your own luck.
14. Focus on the big surprise that awaits you at the end of the journey.

The first step towards change is to be able to know what to focus on particularly the challenge. For me, to remain inspired in this quest, one must not consider it a disability because, by its definition, one's outlook will be overshadowed with dismay and pessimism. Instead, we should replace the word disability with physically or medically challenged, whatever the challenge may be.

The second step would be to research the challenge. There are billions of information available out there that you can find online or in the library that is useful in identifying the illness and its corresponding solutions. As one goes through the process in identifying the disability, one needs to learn with a mind-to-body connection supported by a total commitment to do what it takes to overcome it.

Grieve. It is all right to be upset.

All of us experience grief and loss differently depending on a lot of factors such as age, belief, culture, personality, and experience. In general, there are five common stages of grieving. According to *Elisabeth Kübler-Ross* in her 1969 book On Death and Dying, the five stages of grief and loss are:

> Denial and Isolation
> Anger
> Bargaining
> Depression
> Acceptance

People who are grieving do not necessarily go through the stages in the same order or experience. The stages of grief and mourning are universal, and people may experience the grieving process differently depending on the degree and intensity of the loss.

Mourning typically occurs as a response to an individual's loss of significant matter in one's life, a terminal illness, the loss of a close relationship, or the death of a valued being, human, or animal. We often transcend or alternate our experience of the process in variable sequence before achieving a meaningful acceptance of our loss. Most of us may not be fortunate enough to experience all of the stages of grieving, and yet in our own time, we eventually reach the final stage of accepting grief. Depression or sadness resulting from an illness or loss of a loved one due to death allows us to do a reality check in our lives that we will all undergo the whole cycle of life from birth, illness, aging, and eventually death as part of our journey in this lifetime.

We must always remember that hope will only end when we are dead. Time is the most precious commodity that one can waste. Many people do not experience grief stages in the order stated earlier, but that is normal. One does not have to go through every step of grieving to be able to understand the process. The stages merely serve as a reference for us to know why we undergo confused emotions and uncertain state of mind at times, even if we thought it had been months or years since our loss.

Years ago, I lost my son Miguel Antonio when he was two years and two months old due to accidental drowning in a family pool, and yet even up to this day, I still grieve for his loss. No one can understand the depth of the pain caused by the loss of a loved one or the agony of seeing a beloved family member or a friend undergo the experience of persistent excruciating pain due to cancer or illness except your self. In a time of mourning or grieving, many of our friends share their emotions and often say, "I understand your pain." However, nobody can neither truly understand nor feel the intensity of the pain except you. In dealing with the pain, others may take a couple of weeks to grieve while others take a lifetime. It is all right to be upset and angry. Take it all out of your chest. Yell if you want to or grieve in silence. Please keep in mind that everyone grieves differently. Others will experience their grief more internally and may not cry. It would help if you try not to judge how a person experiences their pain, as each person will go through the process differently in their terms, their own pace, and their own time.

Denial and Isolation

Most people's initial reaction when they learn about the loss of their function due to terminal illness or death of a loved one is to deny the situation's reality. "This can't be happening. It must be a mistake or a joke". It is a normal reaction to rationalize a person's sudden outburst of emotion overwhelmed by disbelief in reality. To process the event, a person may use denial as a normal defense mechanism to slow down or reduce the amount of shock for the unexplained loss to numb the overwhelmed emotions. One will try to deny the fact and sometimes pretend that it does not matter and brush it off as a normal initial response to the pain.

Anger

After denial, one tends to isolate and shield themselves because one becomes wholly overwhelmed and tired from avoiding the facts, and eventually, the feeling of pain and suffering takes over. The pain can be so intense and unbearable that oftentimes, it hits us at the very core of our being, and it drains every ounce of energy in our soul. Somehow, such outbursts of energy transform into anger directed towards anything or anyone on sight, including inanimate objects, friends, or family. Sometimes, we tend to deny the situation to ourselves and focus our blame on others, even to our loved one who does not have anything to do with the loss. We must remember that grieving is a personal process that has neither a time limit nor a singular way to go about it.

When I was a Social Services Director at a nursing facility, patients and their families blame me for everything, including their terminal illness or even their loved ones' death. When a patient is diagnosed with an illness, and a physician was unable to provide a cure for the disease that caused their family member's death, families blame the institution. The reality of it is that they are grieving by channeling their pain towards us. My job was to mitigate the pain by reducing its intensity through sharing pertinent information that may become useful to them, such as arranging a meeting with the family and the physician to discuss the details of their challenge to prepare their mind into accepting the possibilities. People even try to blame God for their misery for allowing it to happen or not being there to help them when they seek His divine intervention. Everything that happens results from someone else's wrongdoing or neglect, and they do not see themselves as responsible for it.

Bargaining

Guilt is the biggest challenge in this process as people tend to react differently than others as they either blame themselves or others for the unfortunate incident. At this stage, there is a partial adjustment from denial to acceptance when a person justifies their actions or inaction by bargaining. One may have partially realized the facts surrounding the event, and yet there is not much they can do now. When someone feels helpless and vulnerable, the typical reaction is often a need to regain control through a series of "if" statements, such as: "if I would have arrived earlier or if I only had my physical check-up earlier this year, if, if .. if..." But nothing would bring back what happened, nor could we ever rewind the past to justify the "if's". This is another version of bargaining. Some of us never call on God or a higher being for help, yet times like this serve as an opportunity to "bargain" with HIM in an attempt to at least alleviate our pain in slowing down the process.

Depression

There are two types of depression associated with mourning. The first type is sadness, then overwhelmed by grief. When someone dies or becomes ill, we worry about coping with the underlying impacts such as separation, hospitalization bills, burial arrangements, etc... Part of our grief is our feeling of helplessness sometimes indirectly related to our loss such as financial issues, lack of time spent with our loved ones, health issues, and other personal matters.

The second type is privacy in showing our emotions. When someone is quiet and wants time to be alone in times of depression, all they need are simple words of sympathy or a mere tap on the shoulder or a warm hug, that makes a difference.

Acceptance

The final stage of grieving is the ability to accept reality as it is. No matter how soon or how long it takes for one to reach this stage does not matter. Some may not be fortunate to reach it as they remain in denial for the rest of the process. Death may be sudden and unexpected, or we may never see beyond one's anger or denial. The few who learn to accept reality remain calm and at peace. But those in denial will experience some form of withdrawal and unhappiness but not necessarily remain in depression as if life itself has ended and will never be the same again. When I learned to accept my son Miguel's death, I experienced peace, forgiveness, and love that still lingers on.

Loved ones who are terminally ill or aging appear to go through a final period of withdrawal. It is by no means a suggestion that they are aware of their impending death, only signs of physical decline may be sufficient reflection of a similar response. A person's silent behavior may imply that limited social interaction is expected. The dignity and grace shown by our dying loved ones may well be their last gift to us. Coping with a loss is ultimately a deeply personal and singular experience. Nobody can help you go through it or understand the emotions that you are going through. But others can be there for you and to give comfort through this process. The best thing you can do is to allow yourself to feel the grief as it comes. Resisting it will only prolong the natural process of healing.

Think positive and create a plan that you intend to commit.

The most common problem with sudden death or illness is a lack of preparation for the incident. However, it is rare for anyone to prepare for something that no one imagine it can occur. It is like preparing for the big earthquake (which may not happen within our lifetime). It is always wise to be ready for anything that may come our way. We can start by developing our mindset. We must learn to practice positive thinking at all times, supported by a feasible plan for the "what ifs" in our life.

Don't be afraid to take baby steps.

It is all right to make mistakes as long as we take action. Everyone is happy where they are for now and hate to make any changes in life. People always think, "if it is not broken, don't fix it." However, if things happen, one is left unprepared, and that is when matters get worse. So, be prepared.

Sleep and rest.

The most common problem of grieving is worrying too much when realistically, there is nothing much that will change even if we keep thinking about the incident or the problem. No matter how much time and energy spent thinking about it, nothing will change the fact. It is what it is, and that will never change. It is best to just relax, walk your dog or perhaps drink a glass of warm milk with an Oreo cookie and get a much deserved rest and sleep because tomorrow is another day. The more the body lacks rest, it is susceptible to reduced immune system as weakness may settle in, bringing the body down into recession and prone to illness, and perhaps depression.

"Exercise and diet".

Yeah right, that is easier said than done, particularly when you suffer from physical or emotional pain. It may be a difficult for everyone with or without any illness to a snap diet because there is something in food that triggers our brain to an undefined satisfaction, so we tend to overcompensate. But, at least we should try harder, and if not feasible, practice short diet and exercises; and get a little sunshine to give the heart, muscles, and bones their much-needed Vitamins and oxygen.

Stretching aids in circulation of the blood. You can do it at your bedside while sitting in a chair. It is essential to find creative ways to exert simple repetitive physical movement and the right exercise that you like and enjoy. Stretching and yoga may be appropriate because they are simple, less stressful for the body, and you can do it at your own time, space, and mood.

Try to be patient as things do not improve overnight. With exercise, we must maintain a healthy diet with lean meat, fish, fruits, and vegetables.

Maintaining a healthy diet contributes to the body's healing. During the healing process, the body has to deal with the skin continually expanding and shrinking. It is important to eat regularly. Small portions more often are healthier than big portions taken less frequently. All the food groups (carbohydrates, fats, and proteins) must be included in the diet. Always consult with your physician and dietician in making plans or changes in your prescribed diet plan.

Believe and trust in God.

Believe it or not, there is a higher being who is in control of this vast universe. There are unspoken rules and matters in life that neither you, myself, and science have the intelligence to comprehend nor the ability to challenge and explain why things happen except to embrace them as faith. Man is so intelligent that he can explain why matters evolve, but everything beyond explanation can only be explained by faith. There is only one powerful, omnipotent, and omnipresent God, who is more powerful than the universe we live in. It will be very complicated to expound on this subject of God and faith as it will take another new book to discuss the subjective and objective reasoning behind it. But if one does not believe there is God, at least believe in something or some being that is more powerful than you are in this lifetime. This is very important in our understanding of life and its evolution and to help us realize that there must be an ending for every beginning.

Growing in a country where 80% of the population are Catholics, I have a deeper understanding of God's faith. To me, meditation and seeking daily guidance from God is my connection between reality and faith. I also found that prayers help me retain an optimistic perspective of life and its challenges that come my way. Meditation for at least an hour gives me inner peace and optimism. Prayer and meditation sets my mind in a mild form of calmness and serenity. If one does not believe in God, one must at least acknowledge the presence of higher spiritual being more powerful than anyone.

In my childhood years, my mother took me to church every Sunday and special holidays. But my understanding of my religion was merely a regular weekly event to remain in close connection with the community. When I got to college, I felt a deeper understanding of my relationship with God. Until my firstborn child died at the age of two, I underwent severe depression and started to question my faith. I rebelled and was angry with life and my relationship with God. Eventually, with time I learned to humble myself before God and accepted His will. Who am I to question His will? Many of you might be experiencing similar feelings of resentment today in your particular health issues, financial and familial issues, or a loved one's death. But I assure you that God is always there for you even though you question His power and existence in this difficult and confusing time of need. He will answer all your questions, just ask and wait patiently. God will answer you, in His time and His way.

Each day, I do my simple "thank you" prayers for all the things He has given me. Deep inside, I know that God is in every one of us. To me, prayers are so powerful, and moving. It makes me happier and contented each day I wake up, and helps me feel calm before I go to sleep.

Read books that provide encouragement and support.

There is a famous saying: "you can only reap what you sow." The mind is similar to a soil on a small pot. Depending on what you put in it, whether it be grass, weed, flower or fruit bearing seed, you can only harvest what you planted. So, if you plant for example crabgrass, do you honestly expect to reap sweet apple? In parallel, a person needs to instill in his brain only the good stuff like positive thinking, knowledge, encouragement, etc... so that the mind will only develop and nurture the good things it was intended for.

Surround yourself with good and honest people who provide support, and friends who share the same thoughts and aspirations. You want friends who share your visions, dreams, and hope. Why waste time on friends who are not in the same page as you are. Choose the right people to surround you, keep the good apples, and stay away from the crabgrass.

In a time when life becomes a challenge and no one is there with you, do not worry. When your world seem upside down and believing your life will never be the same again as you fight illness or disability on your own, think positive. No matter how many friends you have, eventually they will fade away slowly because you will no longer have the energy and the enthusiasm to socialize the way you used to, but this is also the best time to know your real friends.

When you have friends around and if the only topic of conversation was your illness, in due time, even your kind-hearted friends would lose interest in being there for you. It is crucial for you to judge whether your friends are honest with you. Real friends will be there to support you and do anything in their strength to be there for you. It is rare to find real friends, but you will find a few out there.

Speaking from experience, I remember the time when I came back from a vacation where I injured my back, rendering me physically challenged and unable to do simple chores such as laundry, housekeeping, bathroom routine, and shower. My close friends from college whom I hung out with regularly on weekends came by to visit when they heard about my injury.

After realizing the complexity of my injury, some offered help, but sadly that was all "an offer…" Nobody followed through on their kind words. So, I struggled to do things on my own despite the pain and frustration of my inability to move when I lost control of my gross motor skills. I could not believe that of the hundreds of friends I have, none of them even showed an effort to help me in this time of need. I was blessed to have my loving wife Cecilia, and my daughter Ysabel who is an RN-Nurse Practitioner beside me for support and care. In my most challenging time, my family was there for me, and I love them dearly.

It is also good to know that there are people other than family whom you can talk to for counseling, such as therapists and healthcare professionals who gives advise on matters material to your well-being.

When I had cervical stenosis that required posterior laminectomy with fusion surgery, I accepted my fate, and the new life that came with it. It was not easy, but I learned to humble myself as I went through my challenges. During the date of surgery, it was at the height of the COVID 19 virus infection that killed over a million worldwide. To control the spread of infection, the hospital restricted the amount of people it can handle as no family member was allowed at the recovery area except the patient. I have never felt so alone and depressed, thinking that my life was almost over, imagining that, if I do not die from the delicate surgery, the Virus will definitely hit me with a slow and painful death without saying goodbye to my family at the hospital. It was the scariest and the most dreadful three-days of recovery in my life. I felt frustrated because I was not getting better. I thought that the physical and medical challenges brought by the illness would stay with me for a lifetime. There was no remedy or pill to ease my pain. I have always been a good person so asked myself why did this have to happen to me, why is life so cruel. At my hospital bed, I browsed upon a book that read in part… "Science and man's intelligence can explain everything in life, but matters beyond explanation leave it to faith." Whoa… that was exactly what I needed to know. The critical point for us to realize is that our illness is not a punishment of something that we have done in our lifetime. It is a result of how our body was made from the time we were born, unless we introduced it to our body or from injury. Nevertheless, leave our worries for a while and we should learn to enjoy and appreciate everything that is present in our life. *Carpe Diem*, a Latin phrase by Horace that means *"Seize the day"*. Always think that we still have many great things left to enjoy in life that we ignore and must be appreciated today.

I remember coming home from an overseas trip after learning that my little son died. The flight took more than eighteen hours as it felt like the longest and agonizing trip, I didn't sleep, had no appetite, I kept crying to the point that my tears ran dry and my eyes were about to pop out of their socket… then when the plane finally landed. As I walked the seemingly endless path of the airport tarmac… I glanced upon a short distance, the image of my beautiful wife holding the hand of my second child, Ysabel. I noticed that they were both in tears as they approached and hugged me. It felt surreal, like a dream in slow motion and I could not bear the looks of my wife Cecilia who was in deep agonizing pain when she told me that our son, Miguel is now in heaven. What touched my heart instantly was…. my one-year-old little Ysabel's tight hug as she whispered to my ears softly, "My big brother is in heaven now, but don't worry, we're gonna be fine daddy… were gonna be fine". Imagine my little girl sharing a gentle whisper like a sweet message from an angel relaying words of assurance from God. All of a sudden, the burden and the pain just vanished into thin air, like the fine mist from a raindrop that evaporated as it kissed the white roses in my garden on a fine Spring day.

The process of accepting a loss or terminal illness may take a while. It is normal to feel depressed during the process, but you will soon realize that feeling sorry for yourself will get you nowhere. Remember that you still have life to catch on and enjoy. Take the time to realize your strength and what you can still do. Now is not the time to dwell on the past but to concentrate on the things you can still do at present.

Thinking positive is not an easy matter, but it is essential to be enthusiastic about life. In desperate time like this, we have only two choices. Either stay depressed and complain about the loss or try to make the most out of what's left in life. Studies show that cancer patients who think positive live longer than those who are depressed.

Michael, a high school friend I grew up with, lived across the street from my home with his large family. He was very competitive and a high-achiever, athletic, and well-loved in the community. Then, one day he lost his leg from a motorcycle accident that rendered him dependent on a caregiver. Due to his injury at a young age of 25, he felt that he lost his freedom, identity, and faith. Michael drank himself to depression that eventually led to his death at a prime age. Prior to his demise, I tried to reach out and cheered him up like it was before his accident. We talked about silly subjects and reminisce how it was like when we were kids in third grade. Then, as days go by, he slowly refused to talk to me; he did not return my calls until we lost contact for a week. Michael virtually had a choice to snap out of it for a split second and breathe in some life, but he chose not to. If he had only taken a short time to stop, relax and enjoy the little things that remained in his life, his family, and friends who cared about him, maybe he might still be here with us. Looking back, if I could have done better as a true friend, I don't know if the bond of our friendship was strong enough; I guess time alone can tell.

Always remember, never give up.

Life is tough, but you must be tougher. It depends on your character and personality. If you were just like the rest who easily give up when things get rough, think again because, in this lifetime, there are more turbulent times ahead, and you must be prepared to face it head-on. So, be fierce, act tough, and never give up because the best is yet to come.

Nurture yourself

Who is the most precious person in your life? Who do you value most? Your spouse, a partner, your child, or perhaps your parent? I am sure all these people mean a lot to you; otherwise, you would not be naming them. But there might be times when even they can let you down. The only person who can help is you. It may be odd to know, but you will not believe when I tell you that 'you will always be in your own company'. You can be your best critic by being miserable and, at the same time, your cheerleader.

First, you need to take care of yourself and make sure that you can keep yourself as healthy as possible. Naturally, you cannot cure your illness or disability, but you can learn how to live your life to the fullest and relieve your symptoms in the best possible way you can. There is so much you can do to make yourself feel better. We are all different, and not every remedy or therapy will help anybody

with the same health problem. Symptoms can be different, ranging from a runny nose, itchy or weepy eyes, fever, or weakness, to name a few. It is therefore understandable that some remedies will work for some but not for others.

You will hear some people say that they tried so many remedies or therapies, and nothing ever worked. Some treatments take longer to kick in, and it is essential to be patient and observe the changes that are happening to our body. Often the most effective self-help techniques are the simplest ones. Try to imagine throwing all your negative thoughts and all your pain into a garbage bin and send them away, did you feel relaxed for one sweet second? Imagine, you went to Hawaii and you are sitting down under a huge umbrella sipping your favorite fruit punch in the middle of a cool summer day… just for a brief moment you took your mind out for small vacation and you felt like you actually did. This is a technique that I use a lot especially when I get frustrated, instead of anger, I choose pleasure of imagination to appease my mind. The mind can imagine almost anything you wish; you can let your imagination work. The mind is so powerful and yet we are actually using only less than 10% of its potential. It can actually shift from a bad mood to a good mood or vise versa like a light switch if we want to. You might also consider autogenic training, where you will learn to relax by slow breathing, and it might even help you go to sleep faster if you are experiencing Insomnia. Try to find something that you enjoy. Develop an interest or a hobby. You might enjoy reading a good book over a cup of tea by yourself.

It is much easier to work hard at achieving something for which others will appreciate and say… "well done". But, working hard to recover from your illness and expect others say "well done" on your recovery is quite different. Nobody will appreciate your recovery more than you, so you deserve a pat in the back and say to yourself each day…"Well Done". Praise yourself for any little achievement of the day, no matter how small. It helps to place a positive quote on the wall to remind you every time you wake up and before you go to bed: "Live, Laugh, and Enjoy Life"; "Don't Worry, Be Happy"; "You Can Do This!"

Research on the illness and discover ways to deal with it. Enlighten your mind and learn to accept the new information that could change your life. The only way to have a deeper understanding of your particular situation or illness is to identify the problem and learn why it happened and what are the possible solutions. There are several ways to do it, and one of them is by searching the world-wide-web or commonly known as the Internet. To me, it is one of God's special gift to humankind in this particular time and age. It serves as one of the best information source and the most convenient way to find things, period. Nowadays, you can research just about anything on this planet and even beyond the universe. When you look for something or anybody, 99.9% percent chance that it is on the Internet if it exists, otherwise it is not of this world. The second best way is to learn from the past and finally seek help from a higher being known to man as GOD.

Find out as much as you can about your particular health issue. There are tons of alternative therapies and a holistic approach that could help harmonize your energy with a therapist-controlled setting, such as a clinic. When I injured my back, I tried everything to manage my pain. I went through a long list of specialists like my personal physician who recommended that I see a spine and nerve specialist, a chiropractor, a masseur, and an acupuncturist as they all prescribed medication and regimen of diet exercise to follow when I was at home. I was lucky to have my insurance cover the cost, but to those who neither have the finances nor insurance, there are creative ways to explore, and some are found in the resources section of this book.

One of the helpful and yet cost-free way is to consult the specialist through the Internet using search engines like Google, Yahoo, etc… including YouTube by simply typing your issues on the search engine. You will be surprised how much information you find very helpful to you or a patient's particular situation. I consulted with the specialists from the hospitals, physicians, therapists, and other healthcare professionals about the medical and my personal issues, chat with friends and friends of friends through Facebook, and I received helpful hints on what to do. It was inspiring and useful in two ways: I now have a support group, and I do not feel alone anymore, and I have a clearer understanding of my illness and how to deal with it.

There is really no singular cure or solution out there, so you need an open mind to find other available alternatives in your local community. Another option I found was the use of natural herbs and juices to cleanse my internal organs and help reduce the pain. Limitation in finances and resources led me to try creative ways to save money while addressing my back pain issues so, I went online and found a plethora of information ranging from exercises that can be done at home using whatever table, couch, bed, stairs, etc… that one can utilize creatively. The best thing is that they are free.

Chapter 4

Communication with Care Receiver

Many people with learning disabilities have some difficulties with communication, which partially leads to behavior issues. Improving communication may help reduce or stop challenging behavior. Communication is one of the most important ways in which we control our environment and influence other people. If a person's communication skills are restrained, a person may become frustrated and challenging behavior would evolve. If a specific need is met with the use of a form of behavior, whether it be aggression or isolation, the person with a communication barrier or learning disability will perceive it as a means to meet the needs. When this pattern of behavior is regularly observed, the behavior will then be perceived as the norm.

Among individuals with developmental challenge, communication is a significant issue that can be partially attributed to the following difficulties: (a) Difficulties in understanding what other people are saying; and (b). The challenging to process situations where there is too much language to process. (c). Difficulties in understanding abstract concepts (things that cannot be seen or touched), negatives (e.g. "not", don't"), and concept of time (e.g. "yesterday", "this afternoon"). (d). Difficulties in understanding sarcasm and taking things literally (e.g. "Oh, that's great!" when you actually mean the opposite).

Understanding these subjects requires attention to the tone of voice, facial expression, and body language, which the person might not understand especially for people with developmental challenges. Some individuals may find difficulty communicating a message to others due to complications in producing clear speech/sign, lack of words to send the message, and using the right words but in the wrong order or without the appropriate supporting body language.

To help encourage the care-recipient with communication, the caregiver must ensure that they speak, write or use sign language or other ways that the person may understand. This may be achieved using simple, short sentences and avoiding complex words that are hard to comprehend or could be easily misunderstood. The use of objects, pictures, communication board and symbols, sign language, and voice communication device is also a great way to supplement spoken language.

Communicating to people with disabilities.

Individuals are sometimes concerned that they might say the wrong thing to offend people with disabilities, so they say nothing further. Here are some suggestions on how to relate and communicate with people with disabilities.

Respect and courtesy are the most basic appropriate etiquette when interacting with people with disabilities. Positive language empowers. It is essential to put the person first when writing or speak about people with disabilities. Group designations such as "the blind", "the retarded", or "the disabled" are inappropriate because they do not reflect the individuality, equality, or dignity of people with disabilities. Further, words like "normal person" imply that the person with a disability is not normal, whereas "person without a disability" is descriptive but not cynical.

Communicating with Individuals
with Cognitive Disabilities

Be prepared to repeat clearly what you say or write. If you are in a public area with many distractions, consider moving to a quiet or private location. Be patient, flexible, and supportive. Take time to understand the individual and make sure the individual understands you.

Offer assistance in completing forms or understanding written instructions and provide extra time for decision-making. Wait for the individual to accept the offer of assistance; do not "over-assist" or be patronizing.

Communicating with Individuals Who are Blind or Visually Impaired

Tell the individual when you are leaving. Please speak to the individual when you approach him or her. State who you are in a normal tone of voice. When conversing in a group, remember to identify yourself and the person you are speaking to. If you are offering a seat, gently place the individual's hand on the chair's back or arm to locate the seat. Please do not attempt to lead the individual without first asking; allow them to hold your arm and control their movements.

Be descriptive when giving directions; verbally provide the person with the visually apparent information for individuals to see. For example, if you are approaching steps, mention how many levels.

Communicating with Individuals with Speech Impairments

Concentrate on what the individual is saying. Be patient. Take as much time as necessary. Do not speak for the individual or attempt to finish her or his sentences. Try to ask questions which require only short answers or a nod of the head. If you do not understand something that the individual said, do not pretend that you do. Ask the individual to repeat what he or she said and then repeat it back. If you are having difficulty understanding the individual, offer them to write it, but ask the individual first if this is acceptable.

Communicating with Individuals Who Are Deaf or Hard of Hearing

If the individual uses a sign language interpreter, speak directly to the person, not the interpreter. Gain the person's attention before starting a conversation (i.e., tap the person gently on the shoulder or arm). If you telephone an individual who is hard of hearing, let the phone ring longer than usual. Speak clearly and be prepared to repeat the reason for the call and who you are. If you do not have a Text Telephone (TTY), dial 711 to reach the national telecommunications relay service. It facilitates the call between you and an individual who uses a TTY. Look directly at the individual, face the light, speak clearly in a normal tone of voice, and keep your hands away from your face. Use short, simple sentences. Avoid smoking or chewing gum while on the phone.

Communicating with Individuals with Mobility Impairments

If possible, put yourself at the wheelchair user's eye level. Do not lean on a wheelchair or any other assistive device. Do not assume the individual needs assistance. Ask first before doing so. Offer assistance if the individual appears to be having difficulty opening a door. Never patronize people who use wheelchairs by patting them on the head or shoulder. If you telephone the individual, allow the phone to ring longer than usual to allow extra time to reach the telephone.

Communicating with People with Disabilities

Don't be afraid to ask questions when you're unsure of what to do. If you offer assistance, wait until the offer is accepted. Then listen to or ask for instructions. Treat adults as adults. Address people who have disabilities by their first names only when extending the same familiarity to all others.

Relax. Don't be embarrassed if you happen to use common expressions such as "See you later," or "Did you hear about that" that seem to relate to a person's disability. When introduced to a person with a disability, it is appropriate to offer to shake hands. People with limited hand use or who wear an artificial limb can usually shake hands. (Shaking hands with the left hand is an acceptable greeting.)

Points to Remember

- Relax.
- Listen to the individual.
- Treat the individual with dignity, respect, and courtesy.
- Offer assistance but do not insist or be offended if your offer is not accepted.

Chapter 5

Correlation Between Challenging Behavior and Medical Issues Among Individuals with Disability

When an individual is hospitalized regardless of whether it was caused by an accident, lingering illness, cancer, or anything that entails pain, anxiety, and uncertainty, along with, it comes stress and challenging behavior to any normal healthy human being. Frequently, stress is accompanied by an elevation in blood pressure, sweat, and possibly tears that bring along other significant pre-existing conditions. It also triggers one's delicate emotion into a whirlwind of different feelings that could cause a person to react differently, besides being calm in certain unique situations. Imagine when this happens to an individual with limited cognitive and psycho-social abilities or even to a young child. Simple pain or medical condition can be magnified or perhaps even result in an explosive situation.

Understanding Challenging Behavior

During my career as a Social Worker for the Inland Counties and Los Angeles, California, it has always been a challenge and a fascination for me to understand why individuals that are mentally challenged and those with limited cognitive ability often resort to challenging behavior particularly when they undergo pain or have medical issues. Back in the early 1980's, people with learning disabilities or cognitive challenges are considered mentally retarded. Let us be clear that such terminology is unacceptable because it is demeaning and insulting by nature. Challenging behavior can occur to anyone even to normal people including those who have learning disabilities but such is particularly magnified and prevalent among those with psychiatric disorders.

Let us look at what challenging behavior is about. Challenging behaviour is also known as maladaptive behavior, aberrant behavior, refusal to comply, etc. However, it is basically defined as that which is "culturally abnormal behaviour of such an intensity, frequency, or duration that the physical safety of the person or others is likely to be placed in serious jeopardy, or behaviour which is likely to seriously limit use of, or result in the person being denied access to an ordinary community facility" (*Emerson, 1995*). Challenging behavior is often associated with a range of negative personal and social consequences. Such practices may significantly impair the physical and mental health and or quality of life of the person, those who care for them, those who live nearby, and extreme cases may even result in death (*Mukaddes & Topcu, 2006; Nissen & Haveman, 1997*).

However, the consequences of challenging behaviors can go far beyond their immediate physical impact. People with behaviors are significantly more likely to be excluded from community-based services and be retained in institutional settings (*Borthwick-Duffy, Eyman & White, 1987*). People are also expected to be excluded from services provided within these settings (*Oliver, Murphy & Corbett, 1987*). Within the community, challenging behaviors may serve to limit the development of social relationships and reduce the opportunities to participate in community-based activities (*Anderson, Larkin, Hill & Chen, 1992*). Challenging behaviors may also be an obstacle to learning new skills, particularly for those based in school settings (*Chadwick, Piroth, Walker, Bernard & Taylor, 2000*). This in turn, may lead to a coercive trap whereby the individual does not learn different behaviors to replace challenging behaviors. As a result, the individual continues to emit the problem behaviors.

The term 'challenging behavior' is also used to describe a broad class of unusual behaviors shown by individuals with intellectual disabilities. They include aggression, destructiveness, self-injurious behavior (*SIB*), stereotyped behaviors, and a range of other behaviors (*Emerson, 2001*). *Emerson et al.* (2001a) reported that the primary forms of challenging behaviors shown are SIB and aggression, with the prevalence of this increasing into teenage years. Stereotyped behaviors are often viewed as the least problematic of challenging behaviors, receiving less intensive intervention than aggression or SIB or often receiving no treatment at all (*Matson, Benavidez, Compton, Paclawskyj, & Baglio, 1996*). However, engagement in stereotypical behavior also produces negative social consequences, particularly by interfering with skill acquisition and may be a precursor to SIB (*Morrison & Rozales-Ruiz, 1997*).

Researchers have indicated that individuals who display challenging behavior often show more than one form of behavior. *Emerson et al.* (2001a) found that between one and a half and two-thirds of people identified as showing challenging behavior did so in two or more forms. Similarly, *Borthwick-Duffy (1994)* found that from those identified as displaying challenging behavior, 25% did so in more than one of three possible areas, those being aggression, SIB, and property destruction. In addition to the co-occurrence of challenging behavior across two forms, people are also more likely to show multiple topographies of these forms of challenging behavior (*Emerson, 2001*). *Harris (1993)* reported that the most prevalent forms of aggression shown by 168 individuals were punching, slapping, pushing or pulling (51%), kicking (24%), pinching and scratching (21%). The most common forms of SIB shown by people with intellectual disabilities include repeated self-biting, punching or slapping, hitting head against objects, hitting other parts of the body or self scratching (*Emerson et al., 2001b*).

Additional studies have extended the investigation of prevalence and forms of challenging behavior are attributed to other risk factors known as personal and environmental. In relation to gender, boys and men are more likely to be identified as showing challenging behavior than girls and women (*Emerson, 2001*). In a study on physical aggression towards others, *Tyrer et al.* (2006), found a higher prevalence of aggression in men than in women. This mirrors findings by *Oliver et al.* (1987) who found that men are more likely to emit aggressive behaviors and property destruction than SIB. However, many studies have shown that gender is not a risk factor for challenging behavior. *Baghdadli, Pascal, Grisi, & Aussilloux (2003)* reported that SIB concerns nearly half of the children studied without gender effects.

Similarly, *Chadwick et al. (2000)* found no significant differences in any challenging behavior measures (SIB or aggression) taken between boys and girls.

The prevalence of challenging behaviors appears to increase with age during childhood, reach a peak during the age range 15–34, and then decline *(Oliver et al., 1987)*. *Holden and Gitlesen (2006)* found that age is clearly associated with challenging behavior, mainly in that more challenging behavior is common among adults under 40 years, and less challenging behavior is common among adolescents.

Challenging Behaviors prevalent among individuals with a developmental disability.

In general, the prevalence of challenging behaviors is positively correlated with the degree of intellectual impairment. For example, *Borthwick-Duffy (1994)*, found that 7% of people with mild; 14% of people with moderate; 22% of people with severe; and 33% of people with profound intellectual disability show one or more forms of challenging behavior. *Holden and Gitlesen (2006)* reported that challenging behavior increased with the severity of mental retardation. The authors of this study also found that aggression is more common among people with mild and moderate intellectual disabilities, and SIB is more common among people with profound and severe intellectual disability.

The correlation between the diagnosis of cognitively challenge or psychiatric disorder, and challenging behavior is very complicated. However, I would like to simplify the discussion on such a relationship without causing too much confusion. Any form of challenging behavior may occur to anyone, particularly when one has pain or a diagnosis that could affect a person's emotion, psyche, aura, or sensibility. For instance, let us say a diagnosis of terminal illness or pain caused by injury or surgery that impacts a person's mood and being. Challenging behavior can occur to a person with or without any psychiatric disorder diagnosis, and not all individuals with psychiatric or emotional issues have challenging behavior.

However, as part of the criterion for this discussion, some people who have an essential diagnosis of some form of challenging behavior (ie.

self-injury in depression, aggression secondary to persecutory delusions in schizophrenia, and wandering in dementia) which must be indirectly or directly correlated to a medical diagnosis or condition for us to draw a clear presumption connection. Learning disabilities and autistic spectrum disorder may also be present in various combinations of comorbidity.

Epidemiology

There are, however, studies examining the prevalence of specific problem behaviors in adult mental health settings. For example, *Steinart et. al. (1999)*, in a study investigating the prevalence of aggressive behavior in acute in-patient settings, found that 75% of the men in the sample and 53% of the women exhibited some type of aggressive behavior (including harm to self) during their first or subsequent admission. Perhaps aggression is the individual's way of expressing insecurity caused by a new unpredictable environment that is intimidating to them, especially if they do not see familiar faces in a different environment from the original place where they were initially.

Studies have shown that several endogenous substances have been investigated for their role in the development and maintenance of challenging behavior. In particular, opioid peptides (β-endorphins), sex hormones, dopamine, and serotonin have been studied in relation to their role in mediating human behavioral processes such as aggression and arousal self-injury, and appetite. Endogenous opioids have been implicated in SIB's pathophysiology, and a number of aetiological pathways have been hypothesized; for example, the intrinsically rewarding properties of endorphins released by SIB. Serotonin has been implicated in SIB, aggression, stereotypies, anxiety, and behavioral disinhibition. Testosterone has also been implicated in the mediation of aggressive and abnormal sexual behavior. In particular, impulsive aggression in personality disorder correlates with tritiated paroxetine binding in the platelet. All the above-mentioned aetiological pathways have been utilized as the neurochemical basis of pharmacotherapeutic interventions.

Thus, although there are many studies on neurobiological differences between people with psychiatric disorders and controls, there are relatively few related frequency and severity of individual challenging behaviors to particular biological variables. Nonetheless, some progress has recently been made, for example, in understanding the neurobiological correlations of violent behavior.

Qualitative computerized axial tomography (CT) and quantitative positron emission tomography (PET) studies have reported anatomical abnormalities, and reduced glucose metabolism, in prefrontal and temporal regions. The use of proton magnetic resonance spectroscopy (HMRS) to study the neuronal integrity of the prefrontal lobe and amygdala-hippocampal complex in repetitively violent adults and non-violent matched controls. The study found that repetitively violent people had reduced neuronal density and abnormal phosphate metabolism in the prefrontal lobe and amygdala-hippocampal complex; and the degree of reduced neuronal density was related to the *frequency of violence (Critchley et al 2000)*.

The majority of research into psychological factors underpinning the etiology of challenging behavior has taken a functional perspective, with its origins in learning theory. In this approach, the emphasis is on the purpose the behavior serves for the individual, rather than the form of the behavior per se. Alternative hypotheses relating to the functions of the target behavior are developed (functional assessment) and systematically evaluated (functional analysis).

In addition to accessing or avoiding either external or internal events, challenging behavior may also serve as a form of communication. A single challenging behavior can also be multi-functional, and there is an emphasis on internal events and emotion in the modern functional analysis. A classic example is when a developmentally challenged individual, who is non-verbal, repeatedly yells while covering his ears and pokes his ear canals, which to a caregiver appears to be a challenging behavior. However, such actions or gestures, a person may just be trying to communicate or express his frustration or that he has an infection in the audio canal.

Assessment and Treatment of Challenging Behavior

It is unfortunate that most challenging behaviors in the community do not always come to the attention of healthcare professionals. A large proportion of people who exhibit challenging behavior are dealt with by the penal system (e.g. prison rehabilitation or probation service), the educational system (e.g. educational psychologists or special schooling), or social services and the voluntary sector (e.g. supported housing, day and respite care provision). Specifically, in the population with learning disability, challenging behavior can be a significant obstacle to resettlement in the community and a frequent cause of requests for admission or re-admission to the hospital (*Mansell, 1994*). When people with challenging behavior, with or without learning disability, do receive health care, it is usually within the mental health care system - but the particular service model varies in location and treatment methods employed.

Both assessment and treatment constitute integral components of the management of patients with challenging behavior. The two processes may not be easily distinguishable-as continuous reassessment often merges with the treatment procedure. Thus, the setting of the patient's management needs must be carefully considered. Out-patient treatment is the obvious first option, provided that safety issues are taken into account. It has the advantage of treating persons in their natural environment, thereby limiting the problems in the generalization of treatment response from in-patient to community settings. Nonetheless, hospitalization may be indicated because of the frequency and severity of the challenging behavior, and specialist in-patient units offer an effective treatment option for certain groups of people (*Xenitidis et al 1999*).

Management of Challenging Behavior

To prevent complications that may be caused by challenging behavior, the following are five essential points on how to manage it:

1. Management needs to be tailored to the individual person, taking into account the particular behavior and the setting in which it occurs.
2. Multi-agency and multi-disciplinary involvement are necessary. It is essential to gather detailed information about the nature and outcome of previous interventions.
3. Different treatment modalities, i.e. pharmacotherapy, psychological and social interventions, alone or in combination,

may be required. Only one treatment should be introduced at a time.

4. The safety of the person displaying the challenging behavior and of others must be considered carefully. A detailed risk assessment should be conducted, and the degree of urgency of the response decided.

5. If necessary, treatment in a safe and secure environment within the framework of the state and federal regulations.

Whatever the setting and the legal framework, the management of challenging behavior is typically resource-intensive. Often, a single agency may take the lead, but collaboration among a number of agencies will be necessary. Within each agency, several disciplines will need to be involved in both the assessment and treatment phases. The collection of background information from many sources is essential if an accurate formulation of the development of the challenging behavior were to be made, and the risk associated with it minimized.

A detailed review of a patient's medical, educational, and social records is time-consuming but necessary for clarifying the degree of success of previous formulations and interventions. Medical investigations will be required, as appropriate, into the presence of any comorbid medical condition or mental disorder. If a causative association is suspected, the direction of causality should be determined.

Information should be gathered from various sources, including the patient's report, interview with family and caregivers, and direct observation of behavior. Management should be guided by the principles of sequential single hypothesis testing. That is, the challenging behavior should be quantified at baseline, and the effectiveness of each intervention is assessed accurately and reliably, measuring pre- and post-treatment levels. Only one treatment should be introduced at a time, and response to that treatment should be measured before it is replaced or augmented by others. In this way, specific treatments' particular benefits can be evaluated, allowing later refinement of focused service delivery.

Steps Toward Systematic Assessment and
Treatment of Challenging Behavior

There are six steps on how to conduct effective systematic assessment and treatment of challenging behavior:

1. Identification of target behavior(s) Quantitative measurement of the target behavior.
2. Generation of hypotheses (medical, psychological, and social) about the genesis and maintenance of the behavior.
3. Delivery of therapeutic intervention designed to test the theories developed in line with a sequential, single hypothesis-testing model.
4. Evaluation of the effectiveness of the intervention
   Generation and testing of alternative hypotheses.
5. The use of standardized assessment tools facilitates the reliable and accurate measurement of the target behavior.

Several scales exist that provide a comprehensive assessment of challenging behavior domains, for example, the Adaptive Behavior Scale (*Nihira et al, 1974*). However, these were primarily developed for people with learning disabilities and did not apply well to the general adult population. Although each clinical specialty may possess its tailored measures to describe and categorize problems presented in that clinical area (e.g. Body Mass Index in eating disorders), people may also have a number of generic problems that require broader assessment tools (e.g. self-injury or depression). For example, the Overt Aggression Scale (OAS) for the Objective Rating of Verbal and Physical Aggression (*Yudofsky, 1986*) allows verbal and physical aggression to others, self, and property to be evaluated in a clinically applicable format. As noted above, this part of the assessment aims to measure the frequency and severity of the challenging behavior and any putative determining factors objectively.

Pharmacotherapy

The treatment of an underlying mental disorder, epilepsy, or other physical condition should be the target of any specific medication in the first instance. The general principles of pharmacotherapy should follow the principles highlighted in the section on Aetiology that is focused on the medical condition that causes the behavior.

Self-Injury

The opioid antagonists naloxone and naltrexone have been used for the reduction of SIB in learning disability patients. It is thought that this reduction is mediated by a selective blockade of endorphin receptors leading to the removal of the biologically based reinforcing properties of self-injury. There have also been reports on the effective use of serotonergic antidepressants for the treatment of SIB.

Sexually Inappropriate Behavior

Antilibidinal drugs have been used with recidivist sex offenders and other patients repeatedly exhibiting unacceptable or dangerous sexual behavior. The mechanism of antilibidinal drugs' action is thought to be through a reduction of circulating androgens in the bloodstream. As testosterone has been associated with aggressive as well as hypersexual behavior, these drugs may act on both components of complex, aggressive sexual behavior, reducing its manifestation.

Aggression

Although some drugs have been marketed as having a specific anti-aggressive effect, it is more likely that any reduction of aggression is either secondary to a reduction of a primary psychopathology, or results from a non-specific sedative effect.

Psychological Treatments

From a learning theory perspective, *Goldiamond (1974)* outlines two contrasting approaches to assessing and treating problematic behaviors.

The pathological approach views challenging behavior as a problem that has to be suppressed or removed. Although many studies report effective suppression of targeted challenging behavior (e.g., extinction), interventions based on a pathological approach can be described as 'prosthetic'. There are well-established problems with generalization across settings, long-term maintenance, and symptom substitution. The constructional approach views challenging behavior as a successful means of serving a function. It can be seen in an individual whose resources are compromised as a legitimate and logical path to a desired natural consequence, albeit distressing to the person or others. Interventions based on a constructional approach focus on establishing new, less distressing behaviors. It will serve the same function, leading to the same natural consequence.

Behavior Modification

Treatment within a behavior modification framework is based on the systematic analysis and application of reinforcement. Re-enforcement is the process by which new responses are acquired, and existing ones are strengthened. It refers to the procedure of providing consequences for the behavior that increases or maintains the frequency of that behavior. A re-enforcer is defined by its results. Re-enforcement programs can manipulate the schedule, ratio, and nature of re-enforcers. Restructuring the environment to remove significant contingent events may also be viewed as necessary; for example, social relationships associated with addictive behavior patterns may be avoided until the individual feels confident about renewing acquaintances without reverting to former behavior patterns.

Assessment of challenging behavior using functional analysis can help identify individual alternative behaviors that will produce desirable consequences similar to those of the challenging behavior. The person is then encouraged to substitute these alternative behaviors in settings that would usually elicit the target behavior. This is called solution analysis and is a treatment approach to established therapeutic value. For example, it has been demonstrated that functional and subsequent solutional analyses of parasuicidal acts result in fewer parasuicidal behavior incidents and fewer in-patient days than standard therapies (Linehan et al, 1993). The skills inherent in producing alternative behavior may need to be learned/shaped, as they may not be present in the individual's repertoire.

Cognitive-Behavioral Therapy

The cognitive model and its practical application in clinical psychology have allowed psychological interventions to become more targeted in using internally generated material as a focus for treatment. Cognitive-behavioral therapy (CBT) encompasses a wide range of interventions offered to clients within the framework of 'collaborative empiricism'. Behavioral strategies for managing symptoms, thoughts, beliefs, and feelings are perused and examined for relevance and validity. Traditional or 'elegant' cognitive therapy was developed to work either in combination with pharmacotherapy or alone to ameliorate the symptoms of depression in adults. The success of CBT as an effective intervention has encouraged clinicians and researchers to investigate and apply its techniques in a wide range of clinical problems; these include depression (*for a review, see Watkins & Williams, 1998), panic (Clark et al, 1994)*, psychotic symptoms (*Garety et al, 1994)*, and personality disorder *(Nelson-Gray & Farmer, 1999)*. More recently, the efficacy of CBT as a treatment for adults with a mild learning disability has been established (*Lindsay et al, 1993)*, although, to date, sample sizes have been small.

Psychodynamic and Systemic Therapies

Individual, family, and group psychotherapeutic approaches based on systemic or psychodynamic theories have been used to treat challenging behavior, either alone or as an adjunct to other therapeutic modalities. Data on their effectiveness and efficacy are limited, especially in the learning disability field. Although a number of case reports and review articles have been published in recent years, especially in the area of forensic psychotherapy and psychological treatments of people with personality disorders, further research on both the process and the outcome of psychotherapeutic approaches is needed.

Chapter 6

---※·✧·※---

Coping with Life Challenges
and Aggressive Behavior

T his chapter will discuss the caregiver and the patient's role in coping with changes in people's aggressive behavior in correlation to their loss of personal identity and independence brought about by aging and disability. For a caregiver to cope with the needs of the receiver of care, including ways to deal with their behavior, we need to understand two critical things: (1) what causes the behavior and (2) how do we cope with understanding it.

Dealing with aggressive behavior.

We will learn and understand the correlation between aggressive behavior and medical issues among the elderly and individuals with disabilities. The subject will be briefly discussed in passing to simply help us in our role as caregivers. Although the topic is so broad and deep, we will not elaborate in detail the correlation as the matter can be explained further by psycho-analysts and behavior specialists in a totally different spectrum and study which the book does not find any relevance at this juncture. However, we would like to give the caregiver a broad idea of providing proper care, which includes understanding human behavior.

What Is Aggressive Behavior?

Aggressive behavior can cause physical or emotional harm to others, including verbal and physical abuse. Aggressive behavior violates social boundaries. It can lead to breakdowns in human relationships. Sometimes, it can be obvious or secretive as occasional aggressive outbursts are common and even normal in the right circumstances. You should speak to your doctor if you experience aggressive behavior frequently or in patterns.

Engaging in aggressive behavior causes a feeling of irritability and restlessness. One may feel impulsive and find it hard to control his behavior because he does not know which behaviors are socially appropriate and which ones are not. In other cases, one might act aggressively on purpose, for example, using aggressive behavior to get revenge or provoke someone or direct aggressive behavior towards themselves.

It is essential to understand the causes of aggressive behavior to be able to address it.

Causes of Aggressive Behavior

Many things can shape behavior. These can include: physical health, mental health, family structure, relationships with others, work or school environment societal or socioeconomic factors, individual traits and life experiences

One might act aggressively in response to negative experiences, particularly when one gets frustrated. Aggressive behavior may also be linked to depression, anxiety, PTSD, or other mental health conditions.

Health Causes of Aggressive Behavior

Many mental health conditions can contribute to aggressive behavior. These conditions include:

1. autism spectrum disorder
2. attention deficit hyperactivity disorder (ADHD)bipolar disorder.
3. Schizophrenia.
4. conduct disorder.
5. intermittent explosive disorder.
6. post-traumatic stress disorder (PTSD)

7. Brain damage can also limit your ability to control aggression. You may experience brain damage as the result of: stroke, head injury, certain infections and certain illnesses

Different health conditions contribute to aggression in different ways. If one has autism or bipolar disorder, an act of aggression is a manifestation of frustration or inability to speak about her feelings. If one has a conduct disorder, the act of aggression was for a purpose.

How Is Aggressive Behavior Treated?

To work through aggressive behavior, you need to identify its underlying causes. It may help to talk to someone about experiences that make them feel aggressive. In some cases, one can learn how to avoid frustrating situations by changing their lifestyle or career. You can also develop strategies for coping with frustrating situations. For example, you can learn how to communicate more openly and honestly, without becoming aggressive.

Your doctor may recommend psychotherapy to help treat aggressive behavior. For example, cognitive behavioral therapy (CBT) can help you learn how to control your behavior. It can help you develop coping mechanisms. It can also help you understand the consequences of your actions. Talk therapy is another option. It can help you understand the causes of your aggression. It can also help you work through negative feelings.

Personalized care and attention to detail

Success story No: 154

A lot of behavior issues among individuals' disabilities have a direct correlation with their medical health. For instance, let us take some of my favorite clients for the sake of discussion, and for privacy of information, I will change their names, but the rest of the information shall remain as facts.

Jason D is 21 years of age, ambulatory, non-verbal male diagnosed with severe mental retardation, grand mal seizure with history of tuberous sclerosis, ventriculo-peritoneal shunt (VP shunt), mild visual impairment. Jason is a charming young adult who likes interaction and willing to please others with a warm smile. However, he has noted aggressive behavior that is very prominent and predictable at times, particularly when he starts hitting himself in the chest, accompanied by heavy breathing and redness of his face. These are signs that Jason is about to get aggressive. When he gets upset, he yells profanities, throws things that he can grab at people. His staff at home and at his adult daycare program, where he attends daily, evaluated his behavior is cyclical. There are days when he is in a good mood and participates with his staff during program activities. There are days when he is in a bad mood and will continue the rest of the day with several incidences of verbal aggression and physical assault with property destruction. His staff sometimes describes Jason as hallucinating as his behavior appears consistent. During his aggressive spell, he will hold his hands to his ears and screams with profanity. It is sometimes a wonder where he learns those profanities when he is diagnosed with severe mental retardation. During his tantrums, Jason will throw anything that he can get his hands on from small items such as toys and chairs to huge items such as a electronic piano that weights about 100 lbs. It is also notable that his aggressive behavior does not have any antecedent or precedence to warn anybody that he is about to explode literally. In one minute, he will be participating actively without any behavior, and then within a short minute, he will be screaming on the top of his lungs and throwing anything he can find. His day at the day program consists of fun-filled activities formulated towards his needs and wants depending on his mood. He enjoys working with clay/ playdough, listening to music with his head-phone, coloring, and puzzles. He also plays an electronic piano. Sometimes, he uses it as a weapon to throw at others when he gets upset. Despite his limited vision, he learned to separate items such as a play money by color and texture.

He learned a lot of his skills by hand over hand assistance with verbal cues from his staff. Jason appears to be learning well and fast, mainly when he is provided with one-on-one attention. I met Jason after his case was referred to me by his former social worker. One day, I responded to an emergency call from an Administrator of a senior skilled nursing facility. She complained that Jason was inappropriately placed due to his aggressive behavior and uncontrolled yelling and property destruction. Every nurse literally refused to provide care for him due to his aggression. Jason came from several failed placements ranging from a high-level behavior facility to a mental health facility due to his assaultive aggression and destructive behavior. My immediate goal was to conduct an initial contact with Jason, his family, and his behavior team. I received a 30-day notice to terminate services, which expires on the day I received the call. The initial contact was uncertain and stressful because I was responding to an emergency call on a client whom I do not have any written history on and whom I barely know. Due to the emergency circumstances stated, there was no available resource or placement that was willing to take him on the day of my visit.

The typical protocol was to provide an emergency team evaluation and a referral by a Psychiatrist to the hospital in the event that Jason becomes a threat to himself and or to others. From the hospital, he may be placed in a restricted environment to monitor his aggression. But this has a unique circumstance. The emergency team met at 8:30 am Friday, as the group already decided to conduct physical restrain and a heavy dose of medication to calm him down. It took me more than 12 hours to figure out a temporary resource solution to deal with Jason's behavior at the senior skilled nursing facility. Jason's aggressive behavior was relentless and uncontrollable. I was up to my wit's end and almost quit my job that day. So, I read through his records, his nursing notes, physician's communication log, and even called his previous residential care homes where he lived in the past ten years. I still could not find a single clue where to start. I was so tired and stressed out, and after three hours of research and communication with his previous caregivers, there were three crucial information that struck my attention:

The first one was the list of medications that he was taking at that time. Jason was loaded with prescription medications ranging from Cogentin 1mg bid (twice a day) for reduction of antipsychotic side effects, Clonozepam 2mg tid (aka Klonopin) (three times a day) for seizure control, Risperdal 3mg twice a day for reduction of aggressive behavior, Tegretol 100 mg 2 tabs thee times a day for seizure control, Paxil 20 mg 1 tab during morning to reduce aggressive behavior, Colace 100 mg in the morning to prevent constipation, Prevacid 30 mg 1 cap during morning for gastric discomfort.

Second, Jason had a history of frequent grand mal seizures during the past three years.

Third, he has a VP Shunt that has not been drained for more than two years since initial placement, and he has tuberous sclerosis.

I was so baffled by what was bothering him. I kept asking myself what it is that drives this young gentleman from a sweet, charming individual to an aggressive, uncontrollable person without any diagnosis of psychotic behavior or any history of mental health problems.

On a regular day, Jason has a great personality, but there are only certain times when his aggression becomes too uncontrollable. I am not a specialist but, my gut feeling tells me that Jason's aggression is not mental health issue but rather a medical health issue that needed to be addressed. During my initial person-to-person contact with Jason, he kept hitting his head on the wall, kept punching his face and his head, he was uncontrollably aggressive to anyone who comes in close distance, including his parents. I noticed that he had several traces of surgical stitches on his head resulting from his past surgeries and facial scars, possibly due to his self-abusive behavior.

As I worked with a team of health care professionals reviewing and analyzing his medical records, my initial impression when I read the list of medications he was taking, his history and diagnosis, his battle scars on his head struggling with his own issues… I suspected immediately that it was his head that was bothering him besides the side-effects of the medications that was prescribed to address his medical and mental health issues. I felt so bad that Jason is unable to explain or describe what was bothering him on top of all his medical and mental health issues.

So, the team focused on the three crucial issues. The nurse was asked if Jason was prescribed any pain medication to address his pain in the head. Since the client has tuberous sclerosis and VP Shunt, is it possible to request for a lab test and an x-ray of Jason's head to explore possible infection that was triggering his aggression. His parents approved the approach, but in order for the technician to provide an x-ray of Jason's head, he had to remain calm, and the best solution was to inject him with a sedative to put him to sleep, he did.

The following day, I came back to the hospital to follow-up on his status as I found a possible home for his temporary placement. After speaking with the Director of Nursing at the skilled nursing facility, and his team of health care professionals, there was an approval to re-evaluate his seizure as well as Jason's VP shunt which was left undrained for a couple of years. Records show that a VP Shunt was surgically placed, but somehow the notes on his VP shunt was left un-monitored as it fell off the radar. His primary approved the exploration of his shunt, and retained fluids were drained. The following day, it was just a miracle. Jason was so gentle and sweet as a small child again, and there was no sign of recurring aggression for the past three weeks prior to his transfer to a licensed adult group home for the developmentally challenged. Up to this date, it was a puzzle and I can't figure out what we to resolve Jason's issues, whether it was the redaction on medications, the draining of the fluids, or something else.

A few months after his transfer, his behavior miraculously disappeared. His staff continued to monitor his shunt and his seizure activity, which is now within normal range. Jason continued to thrive and has now acquired his independence living in his apartment, gainful employment, and a girlfriend he is about to marry.

Looking back at my research notes on the subject, I remember the following information that I wrote and how I reacted to my gut feeling:

Jason has cerebral shunts commonly used to treat hydrocephalus which is the swelling of the brain due to excess buildup of cerebrospinal fluid (CSF). Medical narratives state that if left unchecked, the cerebral spinal fluid can build up, leading to an increase in intracranial pressure (ICP), leading to intracranial hematoma, cerebral edema, and crushed brain tissue or herniation. The cerebral shunt can be used to alleviate or prevent these problems in patients who suffer from hydrocephalus or other related diseases. Shunts can come in various forms, but all of them consist of a pump or drain connected to a long catheter, the end of which is usually placed in the peritoneal cavity.

The main differences between shunts are usually in the materials used to construct them, the types of pumps used, and whether the pump is programmable or not. The shunt's location is determined by the neurosurgeon based on the blockage type and location, causing hydrocephalus. All brain ventricles are candidates for shunting. The catheter is most commonly placed in the abdomen, but other locations include the heart and lungs. Shunts can often be named after the route used by the neurosurgeon. The distal end of the catheter can be located in just about any tissue with enough epithelial cells to absorb the incoming CSF. Based on this information, Jason possibly had hydrocephalous at one time at his very early age, which surgeons placed a shunt. At that time, the problem was that there were insufficient records of his medical history to conclude other potential causes of his aggressive behavior.

As caregivers, we have the responsibility to explore and see how our client's or relatives' situation was years before the incidences occurred to surmise for other possible alternative cures. In Jason's case, it was discovered that there are several complications associated with shunt placement. The majority of these complications occur during childhood and cease once the patient has reached adulthood.

The common symptoms often resemble the new onset of hydrocephalus such as headaches, nausea, vomiting, double-vision, and alteration of consciousness. Furthermore, the shunt failure rate two years after implantation has been estimated to be as high as 50%.

Besides the shunt, I was concerned about the stated side-effects of the prescribed medications he was taking. His variable medications were to address his seizures, possible psychosis, and psuedo-parkinsonism, muscle contraction. In contrast, the effects are considerable (depending on the individual) and they could cause dry mouth, blurred vision, cognitive changes, constipation, urinary retention and even lead to psychosis.

Some of his medications cause dizziness and unsteadiness, loss of orientation, headache, depression, agitation and sleep disturbances. In medical journals, it was stated that sometimes anti-epileptic medications have been associated with an increased risk of suicidal thinking and behavior. In short, the medications that are intended to help him also contribute to his deeper and sometimes unrelated medical problems, which worsens his condition.

In Jason's case, the shunt was placed when he was approximately a year old and was retained during his adolescent age and was somehow lost track during his teen years. Now that he is 21 years old and several failed placement later, the records on the maintenance of his shunt somehow fell through the cracks and caregivers and health care providers lost track of it and they all forgot when was the last time his shunt was drained. After discovering this recent development, Jason's shunt were drained accordingly and was retained as per physician order. From then on, Jason's shunt is now monitored and drained on a timely manner.

This discovery made a huge impact on Jason's life particularly his aggression which was reduced to zero on record and is doing well at school and at home. Jason was eventually discharged from the hospital after his remarkable recovery. Jason transitioned ultimately from failed placements to homebound where he lived initially with his parents and younger sibling.

Since Jason moved in with his parents and no longer living in an intermediate care facility, the case was transferred from my caseload to another social worker who continued to monitor his progress as an independent adult with developmental disabilities.

The last time I heard is that Jason now has a life of his own, although not so perfect, but at least a life full of promising dreams and zero aggression to self and to others. He will eventually become a responsible member of society, still working on his goal of self-reliance and independence. We wish Jason the best....

Aggressive Behavior Attributed to Lack of Vitamins in the Body

According to a book titled as Natural Healing for Schizophrenia & Other Common Mental Disorders by *Eva Edelm*, vitamins and minerals play an important role in a person's mental health and here are a few of the theories and concepts which serves as an inspiration and perhaps resource for alternative solution to our quest in better understanding our roles as caregivers.

All vitamins and minerals are involved in one or more biochemical pathways and/or physiological actions which influence the function of the human brain. Most vitamin and mineral deficiencies result in psychiatric symptoms in a significant number of people, and in people with psychiatric diagnoses these deficiencies are often associated with more severe symptoms and poorer outcome from conventional treatment. Vitamin and mineral deficiencies may act as an exacerbating factor secondary to malnutrition, alcoholism, etc. or may be a primary causative factor. Either way, optimisation of nutrient levels is in each patients best interest.

Vitamin B1 (thiamine): Thiamine deficiency commonly results in psychiatric symptoms. Nine young men were deprived of thiamine to study the effects of thiamine deficiency. After thiamine deficiency was induced, 5/9 of the men developed marked irritability and depression. (*J Broek. 1957*) Another thiamine deprivation study reported symptoms of fearfulness, agitation and emotional instability. (*RD Williams. 1943*)

In one study, low thiamine levels were significantly associated with reduced mood in women, but not in men, *(Benton D. 1995)* while another study reported thiamine deficient individuals were more anxious and more depressed based on ratings from the Adjective checklist, although not more depressed based on the Frieburg personality inventory scale. (*Heseker H. 1992*) Severe thiamine deficiency induced by chronic alcoholism, referred to as *Wernicke-Korsakoff syndrome*, is well known to be associated with a large array of psychiatric and cognitive symptoms. (*Mann. 2000*)

Thiamine is required for the activity of pyruvate dehydrogenase, which catalyzes the conversion of pyruvate to acetyl-coenzyme A. If activity of this enzyme is impaired, excess pyruvate may be converted into lactate (*H. Wick. 1977*), which can cause anxiety. (*RA Buist. 1985*) Thiamine is also required for other aspects of energy metabolism. (*Mann. 2000*) High doses of thiamine (400 mg) have been documented to inhibit platelet monoamine oxidase activity (*Connor DJ. 1981*), although it is not clear if this is a pharmacological effect due to mega-doses or an effect achieved at normal physiological doses.

Investigations into thiamine status of psychiatric patients have produced mixed results. One study reported 0/36 inpatients with major depression, excluding those with high alcohol consumption, had thiamine deficiency upon laboratory testing, (*Bell IR. 1991*) while Carney reported 30% of 172 and 78% of 74 mixed psychiatric inpatients had low thiamine levels respectively. (MW Carney. 1982) (MW Carney. 1979) 7/12 agoraphobia patients were also found to be deficient in thiamine. (*LC Abbey. 1981*) Given that the one study excluding patients with alcoholism found no patients with thiamine deficiency (*Bell IR. 1991*), the discrepancy of these studies is probably due to thiamine deficiency being largely secondary to alcoholism and malnutrition present in many psychiatric patients. Differing laboratory techniques and reference ranges may also be another issue. Thiamine deficiency should be suspected in the presence of alcoholism and malnutrition.

Vitamin B2 (riboflavin): Riboflavin deprivation study, undertaken with 6 male volunteers, examined the effect of riboflavin deficiency on aspects of personality and behavior. (*Ray T. Sterner. 1973*) Results indicated increased levels of depression, hysteria, psychopathic-deviate behavior and hypomania in riboflavin deficient individuals. Chronically riboflavin deficient individuals were reported to be more depressed based on ratings from the Adjective checklist, although not more depressed based on the Frieburg personality inventory scale. (*Heseker H. 1992*)

Riboflavin is essential to many pathways involved in the metabolism of protein, fats and carbohydrates (*Mann. 2000*) and for the activity some P450 enzymes, involved in the metabolism of selected toxins and medications. (*Rivlin RS. 1996*) Riboflavin is also required for the activity of numerous antioxidant enzymes including glutathione reductase, which regenerates endogenous glutathione. In fact, the activity of glutathione reductase is used clinically and in research as a functional marker for riboflavin status. (*Powers HJ. 1999*) Relating to riboflavins antioxidant function, riboflavin deficiency has been associated with oxidative stress. (*Rivlin RS. 1996*) Major depression has also been associated with oxidative stress which may play a role in its development. (*Bilici M. 2001*)

A small amount of research has investigated riboflavin status in psychiatric patients. Of 36 inpatients with major depression, a significant number where deficient in riboflavin. (Bell IR. 1991) Of 172 consecutive mixed psychiatric inpatients, 27% were deficient in riboflavin (MW Carney. 1982) and 1/12 agoraphobia patients were deficient in riboflavin. (LC Abbey. 1982)

Vitamin B6 (pyridoxine).

A single human volunteer consumed a B6 free diet for 55 days. (*Hawkins WW. 1948*) Depression was a notable symptom which disappeared shortly after B6 supplementation commenced. Lower levels of pyridoxal phosphate, the biochemically active form of B6, are significantly correlated with higher levels of depression. (*Hvas AM. 2004*) Irritability and confusion have also been reported as symptoms of B6 deficiency (*Leklem JE. 1991*) and chronically B6 deficient individuals were also found to be significantly more anxious. (*Heseker H. 1992*). **Pyridoxine** is required as a coenzyme for the synthesis of serotonin, dopamine and GABA. Pyridoxine is also required for carbohydrate metabolism and other aspects of amino acid metabolism. (Mann. 2000) 21/101 outpatients with major depression where found to have B6 deficiency while 14/21 B6 deficient patients displayed numbness, paresthesias and 'electric shock' sensations, typical of B6 deficiency. (*Stewart JW. 1984*) By measuring pyridoxal phosphate levels, 4/7 depressed patients and zero controls where found to be B6 deficient. (*Russ CS. 1983*) A more in depth evaluation of B6 status performed using an enzyme stimulation method revealed all 7 depressed patients and none of the controls were B6 deficient. Of 172 consecutive mixed psychiatric inpatients, 9% were deficient in B6. (*MW Carney. 1982*) Significantly more depressed patients, than other psychiatric diagnoses, where documented to have B6 deficiency (*MW Carney. 1979*) and 6/12 agoraphobia patients were deficient in B6. (*LC Abbey. 1982*) 19/39 women on oral contraceptives were deficient in B6 and when these 19 women where given B6 supplements 16/19 experienced improved mood. (*Adams PW. 1973*)

Folate: Depression is a common symptom of folate deficiency. (*JE Alpert. 1997 & Howard JS. 1975*) Of 1081 young men, those who were folate deficient were significantly more depressed based on ratings from the Adjective checklist, although not more depressed based on the Frieburg personality inventory scale. (*Heseker H. 1992*) Two more studies reported a significant association between folate level and depression ratings (*Sachdev PS. 2005*) (*Bell IR. 1990*), however, another investigating a group of 5948 subjects found no significant correlation between folate levels and depression or anxiety. (*Bjelland I. 2003*) The duration of current depressive episodes was also inversely correlated with serum folate levels in one study, which could be a reflection of dietary practices changing over the course of the illness. (*Levitt AJ. 1989*) Central nervous system abnormalities were found in two thirds of patients with megaloblastic anaemia due to folate deficiency with affective disorder being the most common association. (*Shorvon SD. 1980*). **Folates** basic functions include methylation and DNA synthesis. (*Mann. 2000*) S-adenosylmethionine (SAMe) and tetrahydrobiopterin (BH4), both involved in monoamine synthesis, are lower in the presence of folate deficiency. (*Young SN. 1989*) (*Bottiglieri T. 1992*) Lower central nervous system levels of 5-hydroxytryptamine (serotonin) are also documented in folate deficiency. (*Young SN. 1989*) The most likely explanation for the association between folate status and psychiatric symptoms is its connection with monoamine metabolism via methylation, although other functions are also likely relevant. High plasma homocysteine levels have been shown to correlate strongly with low cerebrospinal fluid levels of folate, SAMe and monoamines. (*T Bottiglieri. 2000*) Homocystine levels are not raised in all cases of folate deficiency, so are not reliable marker for folate status. If elevated homocysteine levels are an innocent marker for folate, B12 and other deficiencies, or if elevated homocysteine also plays a direct role in major depression and anxiety disorders is unclear. *(Bottiglieri T. 1996)* Anemia and macrocytosis can be the result of folate deficiency, although they are only present in more severe cases so are also not a reliable predictor of folate status in psychiatric populations. *(Mischoulon D. 2000)*

A large body of research has examined the status of folate in psychiatric patients. 9/12 studies summarized below found folate deficiency in 17-31% of patients. The discrepancy between these 9/12 studies which reported high rates of deficiency and 3/12 studies reporting low rates, 0-3.4 %, is likely explained by different diets, alcohol consumption, laboratory techniques and reference ranges.

A prospective study followed 2,313 men aged between 42 and 60 for over 10 years. *(T Tolmunen. 2004)* At the beginning of the study, individual's diets were analysed and divided into below and above the energy-adjusted median folate intake. Those below the median folate intake level had a relative risk of 3.04 (CI: 1.58-5.86) of receiving a diagnosis of depression.

Low serum folate levels were associated with a higher relapse rate in people with major depression being treated with fluoxetine. *(Papakostas GI. 2004)* In another study, high folate levels predicted greater improvement via SSRI's in 22 depressed patients over 60 years old. (Murray. 2003) Low serum levels of 5-MeTHF, a biologically active form of folate, are not predictive of response to electroconvulsive therapy (ECT) in major depression. *(Wilkinson AM. 1994)*.

Vitamin B12 (cobalamin): Depression is a common early psychiatric manifestation of B12 deficiency. *(Durand C. 2003 & Goodman KI. 1990 & Hector M. 1988)* Other symptoms include mania and psychosis, (Hector M. 1988) and slowing of mental processes, confusion and memory defects. *(Holmes JM. 1956)* Of 1081 young men, those who were B12 deficient were significantly more anxious based on ratings from the Adjective checklist, although not more anxious based on the Frieburg personality inventory scale. *(Heseker H. 1992)*. **B12** is a cofactor required for methionine synthase, which catalyses the conversion of homocysteine to methionine *(Bottiglieri T. 1996)*, and is required for the production of energy from fatty acids and proteins. (*Mann. 2000*) Methionine is the direct precursor of S-adenosylmethionine (SAMe), which is involved in methylation reactions including neurotransmitter synthesis. B12 deficiency also causes folate to be 'trapped' in a form not available to perform its function. (*Mann. 2000*)

In one study, 47 patients with depression underwent high-resolution magnetic resonance imaging scans and B12 levels assessment. (*Hickie I. 2005*) Low B12 levels were found to be predictive of white matter lesions. Of 50 patients with B12 deficiency associated megaloblastic anaemia, 26% displayed organic mental changes and 16% had subacute combined degeneration of the spinal cord. (*Shorvon SD. 1980*) 8/9 patients with B12 deficiency and the absence of hematologic evidence of deficiency displayed abnormal evoked potential, evidence of electrophysiologic neurological impairment, while selected individuals had myelopathy, neuropathy and seizure disorders. (*Karnaze DS. 1990*) Low B12 status is associated with low RBC and WBC in psychiatric inpatients. (*Carney MW. 1978*) These haematological abnormalities are predictive of low B12, although their presence or absence does not confirm or rule out B12 deficiency. B12 deficiency has a major and well documented negative effect on neurological function.

A number of studies have investigated the presence of B12 deficiency in psychiatric populations. The discrepancy between different studies is likely explained by different diets (e.g. animal product consumption), laboratory techniques and reference ranges. The rate of deficiency varied between 3.7 and 26.1 %.

In psychiatric patients, low B12 levels correlate highly with depression rating scores (*Levitt AJ. 2003*) and, in healthy volunteers, those with chronically low B12 levels have significantly higher depression levels. (*Heseker H. 1992*) Other studies have not confirmed these associations. In a group of 5948 subjects aged 46 to 49 years, depression ratings, anxiety/depression ratings and B12 levels were assessed. No significant correlation was found between B12 levels and depression and anxiety. (*Bjelland I. 2003*) Another study of 412 persons aged 60-64 years also found no significant association between B12 levels and depression ratings. (*Sachdev PS. 2005*) Several studies have confirmed depressive patients who also had symptoms of psychosis tend to have lower B12 levels than depressive patients with no psychotic symptoms. (*Bell IR. 1991 & Bell IR. 1990*) Of 84 patients with megaloblastic anaemia, 50 had B12 deficiency. Of these 50 patients 20% had an affective disorder. (*Shorvon SD. 1980*)

In patients with major depression, higher B12 levels have been associated with improved treatment outcomes in one study (*Hintikka J. 2003*) while another using fluoxetine as the treatment agent found no association between B12 levels and treatment outcome. (*Fava M. 1997*)

Vitamin C (ascorbic acid): Depression is a classic early symptom of vitamin C deficiency. (*Robert E. 1971*) In a vitamin C deprivation study, symptoms of depression, hypochondriasis, hysteria, reduced arousal and reduced motivational were documented. (*Robert A. 1971*) In a study of 1081 young men, those who were vitamin C deficient were significantly more anxious and people deficient in vitamin C were also significantly more depressed based on ratings from the Adjective checklist, although not more depressed based on the *Frieburg personality inventory scale*. (*Heseker H. 1992*). **Vitamin C** is a cofactor for dopamine beta-hydroxylase (*Kaufman S. 1966*), which is involved in the conversion of dopamine to norepinephrine, and a cofactor for tryptophan-5-hydroxylase required for the conversion of tryptophan to 5-hydroxytryptophan (*Cooper JR. 1961*) in serotonin production. Vitamin C also has broad-spectrum antioxidant properties and is essential for the mitochondrial metabolism of fats. (*Mann. 2000*)

A group of patients depressed for 2-5 months had significantly reduced levels of vitamin C as compared to the non-depressed control group. (*Singh RB. 1995*) Another group of 885 patients in a psychiatric hospital had significantly lower vitamin C levels than controls, reporting 32% had readings below the range in which negative health effects have been clearly documented. (*Schorah CJ. 1983*) A group of chronic mixed psychiatric patients required a longer time period to achieve vitamin C saturation upon supplementation, suggesting lower vitamin C status. (*G Milner. 1963*) Another study reported over 10% of 465 psychiatric inpatients had markedly delayed vitamin C saturation indicating some degree of vitamin C insufficiency. (*Leitner ZA. 1956*)

Magnesium: Magnesium deficiency can cause depression, behaviour and personality changes, apathy, irritability and anxiety. (*Wacker WE. 1968 & Freyre AV. 1970 & Rasmussen HH. 1989*). **Magnesium** is required by over

300 chemical reactions in humans. (*Shils ME. 1999*) Individuals with low cerebrospinal fluid levels of magnesium tend to have lower cerebrospinal fluid levels of 5-hydroxyindoleacetic acid (5-HIAA), a metabolite of serotonin, indicating lower central nervous system serotonin levels. (*Banki CM. 1985 & Banki CM. 1986*) An animal study in which magnesium deficiency was induced in cows found magnesium deficiency was associated with reduced dopamine levels in the cerebral cortex and cerebellum and lower norepinephrine in the corpus striatum. (*McCoy MA. 2000*) The relevance of these findings to human magnesium deficiency is unclear. In humans, magnesium deficiency impairs the cardiovascular response to stress, while stress also increases magnesium requirements. (*Seelig MS. 1994*) Magnesium deficiency also leads to impaired glutamatergic transmission via NMDA-receptors (*Siwek M. 2005*) and an increase in the lactate to pyruvate ratio (*RA Buist. 1985*), both of which are relevant to psychiatric conditions.

Studies of plasma/serum magnesium levels in psychiatric patients have been mixed. In one study, plasma magnesium levels were significantly lower than controls and increased as patients showed clinical improvement. (*Frizel D. 1969*) Three other studies reported lower plasma levels than controls (*Zieba A. 2000*) (*Kirov GK. 1990*) (*Frizel D. 1969*), one study reported no differences (*Manser WW. 1989*) and three others found higher levels of plasma or serum magnesium in non-medicated depressed patients. (*Widmer J. 1992*) (*Cade JF. 1964*) (*Hasey GM. 1993*) Only 1% of magnesium in the human body is present in extracellular fluids (e.g. plasma/serum), making plasma/serum magnesium levels an unreliable marker for magnesium status. (*Mann. 2000*) A group of researchers examining plasma magnesium levels in psychiatric patients found no correlation between low plasma magnesium and increased anxiety levels. (*Kirov GK. 1994*) However 22.4% and 10.4% of patients had levels below and above the laboratory reference range respectively. There was a strong tendency for more disturbed and excitable patients to fall into either the abnormally low or high groups, suggesting a possible significance of impaired magnesium homeostasis.

Two studies found patients with major depression and affective disorders, respectively, showed no significant differences in RBC magnesium levels as compared to healthy controls. (*Kamei K. 1998*) (*Ramsey TA. 1979*) Another study reported 45 depressed patients had lower RBC magnesium levels than 31 controls (*Rybakowski J. 1989*), while another found higher levels of RBC magnesium in non-medicated depressed patients. (*Widmer J. 1992*) A study of more than 200 patients with depression and/or chronic pain documented 75% had below normal magnesium levels in white blood cells. (*Shealy CN. 1990*)

Cerebrospinal fluid (CSF) levels of magnesium were found to be lower in patients with major depression (n = 16) and adjustment disorder (n = 10), as compared with controls. (*Banki CM. 1985*) This research group also found that it was the psychiatric patients with a history of suicide attempts which had low CSF magnesium levels, pulling down the group average. Differences between depressed patients with no history of suicide attempts and healthy controls were insignificant. Another study by this same research group of 275 drug-free psychiatric patients confirmed both of these findings. (*Banki CM. 1986*) Levine and colleagues found an elevated Ca/Mg ratio in the CSF of depressed patients. (*Levine J. 1999*)

Zinc: Psychiatric manifestations of zinc deficiency include behavioral disturbances, depression and mental confusion. (*Mann. 2000*) Within major depression populations, lower zinc levels correlate with higher depression severity. (*Maes M. 1994*). Zinc plays a role in catalysing, and/or is an active constituent of, over 150 enzymes in humans. (*Mann. 2000*) Zinc is involved in such functions as antioxidant defense, gene expression, nerve impulse transmission, thyroid function, digestion and a large array of other functions. Zinc is found in high concentrations in hippocampal and cortical neurons. (*Nowak G. 1998*) Zinc is also an inducer of brain derived neurotrophic factor (*Nowak G. 2005*), is an antagonist of the NMDA-receptor (*Nowak G. 2005 & 2001*) and is required for GABA metabolism. (*Nowak G. 1998*) Zinc deficiency causes biological membranes to be more prone to oxidative damage and impaired function. (*O'Dell BL. 2000*) In one study of six young men, experimentally induced zinc deficiency was shown to reduce basal metabolic rate ~9% and also significantly reduced protein utilization. (*Wada L. 1986*)

Three consecutive studies by *Maes* and colleagues found serum zinc levels were significantly lower in depressed patients as compared to healthy matched controls. (*Maes M. 1994, 1997 & 1999*) Lower serum zinc was associated with higher past treatment resistance. (*Maes M. 1997*) In a group of 30 patients with mood disorders, 7/30 had a clear zinc deficiency. (*Little KY. 1989*) 14 patients with primary affective disorder were found on admission to hospital to have lower plasma zinc levels than 14 controls. *(McLoughlin IJ. 1990)* Another study reported slightly lower plasma zinc levels in depressed patients, although this did not reach statistical significance. *(Narang RL. 1991)*

Nowak and colleagues investigated zinc concentrations of 10 suicide victims compared to 10 age-matched controls. *(Nowak G. 2003)* Hippocampal or cortical tissue showed no differences in zinc content between groups although there was a 26% decrease in the inhibition by zinc of [(3)H]MK-801 binding to NMDA receptors in hippocampal tissue, but not in cortical tissue.

The Benefits of Beet Root Juice

Do you know which health benefits are provided by Beetroot Juice?

Beetroot juice is a deep reddish colored liquid, which is well known for its amazing heath benefits. Beetroot (also known as "beet") is little bit hard to digest but it provides various types of health benefits ranging from blood purification to digestive help. Beetroot juice has great liver cleansing property. It is more nutritious juice termed as the new 'super food'. Beetroot juice is very good for health and regular drinking of beetroot juice helps you to stay healthy.

Beetroot juice is good source of essential nutrients for example important vitamins and minerals. It is rich in folate, vitamin C, and potassium. For achieving maximum health benefits, blend is prepared by incorporating some vegetables to beetroot juice. The juice of beet has a bad taste but it provides so many benefits to health. Nowadays, beetroot juice has become popular due to its stimulating effect to defend against general weakness and some specific diseases.

Some new researches have proved that physiological effects of beetroot juice could help elder people having heart or lung-conditions to live more active life. Beetroot juice also helps athletes to improve their performance. Other recent studies have also revealed that beetroot juice could enhance the flow of blood to the brain that is linked to cognitive health so it may be helpful to treat dementia.

Beetroot juice Nutrients: Beetroot juice is full of nutrients along with its beautiful red color. Here, nutrient data of beetroot juice is provided.

- Vitamins: It is an excellent source of vitamin C and folic acid. Also, it contains vitamin B1, vitamin B2, vitamin B3 and vitamin A in small amount.
- Minerals: Beetroot juice is high in phosphorus, calcium, potassium, magnesium, and sodium. Also, it contains smaller amounts of manganese, zinc, iron, copper, and selenium.
- Amino Acids: Raw beets are almost consisted of water and carbohydrate but small amounts of amino acids (protein) are also present in it.
- Antioxidants: It also contains flavanoids and carotenoids which can help to decrease the oxidation of LDL cholesterol. When LDL cholesterol gets oxidized, it may cause damage to artery walls, strokes and heart attacks.
- Calories: One beetroot of size 2" (5cm) provide 35 calories.
- Silica: It is rich in silica which is helpful for perfect consumption of calcium in the body. Also, it is necessary for healthy hair, bones, skin, and nails.
- Anti-carcinogenic Color: Betacyanin, an anti- carcinogenic compound provides deep red color to beetroot. It is also helpful to prevent occurrence of colon cancer.

Beetroot Juice Recipe: Beetroot juice has a very strong flavor so before drinking, it should be mixed with other juices for example apple, carrot, and lemon.

Most popular blends of Juice:

Beetroot juice with pineapple and cucumber (best cleansing drink when taken on an empty stomach)

Organic beetroot juice with monin caramel syrup

Blend of beetroot, pineapple, ginger, and cucumber with water

Beetroot juice with apple juice and carrot juice (for boosting energy levels)

Beetroot juice with celery and carrot (for a sweetening purpose, you can add 2 apples in place of the carrots)

Health Benefits of Beetroot Juice:

Heart Health:

Beetroot Juice is very good to improve the health of heart as it increases the good cholesterol level and decreases the bad cholesterol level. So, risk of stroke or heart attack is decreased. Also, it contains nitrate which carry out expansion of the blood vessels so more oxygen and blood is supplied to heart. Also, it decreases the risk of several heart diseases. Its nitrate content also helps to reduce blood pressure so it is considered to be the inexpensive and easiest way to combat hypertension.

Blood Purifier:

Beetroot juice is rich in iron which helps to purify blood and improve the thickness of blood. Also, it improves the blood quality and so solves all problems connected with bad blood such as less hemoglobin and anemia.

Combat Inflammation:

It fights against inflammation and so may be beneficial for obese people in whom inflammation is a risk factor for type 2 diabetes, cardiovascular disease and cancer. Beetroot juice may also be helpful to fight against free radicals.

Disease prevention:

Daily drinking of beetroot juice is also helpful to prevent variety of disease such as dysentery, constipation, piles, gout, diarrhea, vomiting, skin diseases like acne, dandruff, and inflammation, circulatory diseases like hypertension and varicose veins, and birth defects in babies and others.

Other benefits of Beetroot Juice:

Beetroot juice is helpful to increase the stamina. Also, reduces the uptake of oxygen in your body which helps to decrease the weakness level of the body. Daily consumption of beetroot juice can also help to clear of varicose veins. Beetroot juice has an alkaline nature which helps to combat acidity. So, when you suffer from acidosis, take a glass of beetroot juice. It is rich in Vitamin B which plays a direct role to prevent the birth defects in babies so it is very good for expecting mothers.

It is consisted of carbohydrates in natural sugar form so it is good source of fiber. Fibers are relevant to the digestive health and also play an essential role to prevent and treat diseases like piles, jaundice, diarrhea, hepatitis, constipation, vomiting and nausea.

Inorganic calcium deposits can be dissolved in the body by intake of beetroot juice. So, it is helpful to prevent circulatory disorders like varicose veins, arteriosclerosis, hypertension, etc.

Also, it contains tryptophan which produces a well being sense among people. Beetroot juice is a great liver detoxifier as it contains choline. The liver functions become healthy as it contains betaine, the bioactive agent. After the proper functioning of liver, it breaks down the fats, prevents nausea and fatigue, and helps in weight loss.

Beetroot juice offers cleansing properties so it is helpful to treat gout. It is a natural remedy for sexual weakness, for problem of gall bladder and liver.

In some cases, your doctor may prescribe medications to treat your aggressive behavior. For example, they may prescribe antiepileptic drugs (AEDs), such as phenytoin and carbamazepine. If you have schizophrenia, Alzheimer's, or bipolar disorder, they may prescribe mood stabilizers. They may also encourage you to take omega-3 fatty acid supplements.

Treatment plan will vary, depending on the underlying causes of the aggressive behavior. Speak with your doctor to learn more about your condition and treatment options.

Chapter 7

Dementia and Alzheimers

Dementia is described as part of a group of symptoms affecting memory, thinking, and social abilities severely enough to interfere with a person's daily life regardless of age. It is not a specific disease, but there are several different diseases that may cause or related to Dementia. Dementia generally involves memory loss, but memory loss has various causes. Loss of memory alone does not mean a person has Dementia.

Alzheimer's disease is the most common cause of progressive Dementia in older adults. Still, there are several causes of Dementia. Depending on the cause, some dementia symptoms may be reversible.

Symptoms of Dementia

Dementia symptoms vary depending on the cause, but common signs and symptoms include:

A. Cognitive changes. Memory loss, which is usually noticed by a spouse or someone else.

    1. Difficulty communicating or finding words.
    2. Difficulty with visual and spatial abilities, such as getting lost while driving.
    3. Difficulty reasoning or problem-solving.
    4. Difficulty handling complex tasks.
    5. Difficulty with planning and organizing.

6. Difficulty with coordination and motor functions.
7. Confusion and disorientation.

B. Psychological changes.

1. Personality changes
2. Depression.
3. Anxiety.
4. Inappropriate behavior.
5. Paranoia.
6. Agitation.
7. Hallucinations

When you see any of these signs, including memory loss or other Dementia symptoms, bring a loved one or your patient to a doctor as soon as possible. Some treatable medical conditions can cause dementia symptoms, so it is crucial to determine the underlying cause.

I remember my grandmother who was 90 years old then, diagnosed with Dementia as she spent a lot of time recalling her experience when she was 30. What was ingrained in my memory the most was her vivid recollection even of the most minute detail and sequence of her experience as she kept repeating the same stories and words like it just happened yesterday. However, she always referred to me as her youngest son instead of her grandson. I never corrected her about her perception of who I was or reminded her about the same stories she told me almost daily. What mattered most was for her taking the time to call my attention and re-narrating her old repeated stories almost daily. I figured that in her mind, I was her son, whom she cherished when she was younger. I felt guilty somehow for not reminding her that the son she was referring to me died years ago. I felt that it was better that I remain who I was in her mind because it gave her comfort not to remember the sad day when her son passed a tragic death. With her failing health, it was best for my grandmother to remember all those happy years in her life, remembering the good times and the fun times she had.

I enjoyed those precious moments when she just smiled and cheered up as she looked at her old photo albums while I played her favorite vinyl record practically every day. Each day, she sang her heart away to the tune of her favorite Frank Sinatra song... "My Way". Even during the last few days she spent with us, I enjoyed listening to her songs, we laughed at the same jokes. We cherished those precious smiles until one day my grandmother never woke up from her deep sleep smiling as if she has reunited with God and people she knows.

Challenging behaviors associated with Dementia

Dementia can be a devastating diagnosis. The inherent problems with memory, thinking, language, and judgment are a challenge. Still, there are also "behavioral and psychological symptoms of dementia" (BPSD), including agitation, aggression, wandering, resistance to care, delusions, hallucinations, and repetitive speech that may come along. These symptoms can be very upsetting for people with Dementia and their loved ones and are often the reason people are in long-term care.

Often, doctors prescribe medications, including antipsychotics, antidepressants, and anti-anxiety drugs to help calm patients. There are also problems associated with drug use, including side effects that can lead to serious health issues. Recent evidence recommends a shift in the way we manage challenging symptoms of Dementia, valuing non-drug approaches that calm and reassure people as a first treatment step. The subject of Dementia and Alzheimer's Disease is complex and sensitive to the aging and the cognitively challenged that we will discuss in more detail in the following chapter.

Considering the rapid growth rate of Dementia and the toll it takes on individuals, families, caregivers and healthcare systems, it explains why experts are intensely focused in exploring and testing new treatments and therapies. Non-drug approaches not only avoid the side effects of medication, but there is also increasing evidence that they help reduce challenging behaviors associated with Dementia, making life a bit easier for people with Dementia and their caregivers.

The most common form of treatment to address behavior in Dementia

One: Person-Centered Care. One of the most promising approaches involves an individualized person-centered care model in which a person's background, likes, dislikes, values, culture, and abilities are taken into account to develop communication and care strategies that encourage positive responses and interactions.

Two: The Healing Power of Touch. There are various sensory stimulation types, such as hand massage, which can help improve behaviors and the general well-being of people with Dementia.

Three: Music and Relaxation. Many people enjoy the uplifting and relaxing qualities of music. Relaxing music promotes cooperation during meal times. Listening to music of their choice while receiving one-on-one personal care such as bathing may also help improve behavior among people with Dementia who are more resistant to care. Similarly, receiving five or more sessions of a music-based therapeutic strategy can reduce depression symptoms and improve overall behavioral issues in people with Dementia who are living in long-term care settings.

Other drug-free strategies currently being studied for their impact on agitation among nursing home residents include bright light therapy, doll therapy, pet therapy, and aromatherapy.

Causes of Dementia

Dementia is caused by damage to or loss of nerve cells and their connections in the brain. Depending on the brain's area that is affected by the damage, Dementia can affect people differently and cause different symptoms. Dementias are often grouped by what they have in common, such as the protein or proteins deposited in the brain or the part of the brain that is affected. Some are caused by a reaction to medications or vitamin deficiencies.

Types of Progressive Dementia

Types of dementias that progress and are not reversible include:

A. **Alzheimer's disease.** Alzheimer's disease is the most common cause of Dementia. Although not all causes of Alzheimer's disease are known, experts know that a small percentage is related to mutations of three genes are passed down from parent to child. While several different genes are probably involved in Alzheimer's disease, one important gene that increases risk is apolipoprotein E4 (APOE). Alzheimer's disease patients have plaques and tangles in their brains. Plaques are clumps of a protein called beta-amyloid, and tangles are fibrous tangles made up of tau protein. It's thought that these clumps damage healthy neurons and the fibers connecting them. Other genetic factors might make it more likely that people will develop Alzheimer's.

B. **Vascular Dementia.** This second most common type of Dementia is caused by damage to the vessels that supply blood to your brain. Blood vessel problems can cause strokes or damage the brain in other ways, such as by damaging the fibers in the white matter of the brain. The most common symptoms of vascular Dementia include difficulties with problem-solving, slowed thinking, focus and organization. These tend to be more noticeable than memory loss.

C. **Lewy body Dementia.** Lewy bodies are abnormal balloon-like clumps of protein that have been found in people with Lewy body dementia, Alzheimer's disease, and Parkinson's disease. This is one of the more common types of progressive Dementia. Common signs and symptoms include acting out one's dreams in sleep, seeing things that aren't there (visual hallucinations), and problems with focus and attention. Other signs include uncoordinated or slow movement, tremors, and rigidity (parkinsonism).

D. **Frontotemporal Dementia.** This is a group of diseases characterized by the breakdown (degeneration) of nerve cells and their connections in the frontal and temporal lobes of the brain, the areas generally associated with personality, behavior and language.

Common symptoms affect behavior, personality, thinking, judgment, and language, and movement.

E. **Mixed Dementia.** Autopsy studies of the brains of people 80 and older who had Dementia indicate that many had a combination of several causes, such as Alzheimer's disease, vascular Dementia and Lewy body dementia. Studies are ongoing to determine how having mixed Dementia affects symptoms and treatments.

Other disorders linked to Dementia

F. **Huntington's disease:** Caused by a genetic mutation, this disease causes certain nerve cells in your brain and spinal cord to waste away. Signs and symptoms, including a severe decline in thinking (cognitive) skills, usually appear around age 30 or 40.

G. **Traumatic brain injury (TBI).** This condition is most often caused by repetitive head trauma. People such as boxers, football players or soldiers might experience TBI. Depending on the part of the brain that's injured, this condition can cause dementia signs and symptoms such as depression, explosiveness, memory loss and impaired speech. TBI may also cause parkinsonism. Symptoms might not appear until years after the trauma.

H. **Creutzfeldt-Jakob disease.** This rare brain disorder usually occurs in people without known risk factors. This condition might be due to deposits of infectious proteins called prions. Creutzfeldt-Jakob disease usually has no known cause but can be inherited. It may also be caused by exposure to diseased brain or nervous system tissue, such as from a cornea transplant. Signs and symptoms of this fatal condition usually appear after age 60.

I. **Parkinson's disease.** Many people with Parkinson's disease eventually develop dementia symptoms (Parkinson's disease dementia).

Dementia-like conditions that can be reversed:

Some causes of Dementia or dementia-like symptoms can be reversed with treatment. They include:

1. Infections and immune disorders. Dementia-like symptoms can result from fever or other side effects of your body's attempt to fight off an infection. Multiple sclerosis and other conditions caused by the body's immune system attacking nerve cells also can cause Dementia.
2. Metabolic problems and endocrine abnormalities. People with thyroid problems, low blood sugar (hypoglycemia), too little or too much sodium or calcium, or problems absorbing vitamin B-12 can develop dementia-like symptoms or other personality changes.
3. Nutritional deficiencies. Not drinking enough liquids (dehydration); not getting enough thiamin (vitamin B-1), which is common in people with chronic alcoholism; and not getting enough vitamins B-6 and B-12 in your diet can cause dementia-like symptoms. Copper and vitamin E deficiencies also can cause dementia symptoms.
4. Medication side effects. Side effects of medications, a reaction to a medication or an interaction of several medications can cause dementia-like symptoms.
5. Subdural hematomas. Bleeding between the surface of the brain and the covering over the brain, which is common in the elderly after a fall, can cause symptoms similar to those of Dementia.
6. Poisoning. Exposure to heavy metals, such as lead, and other poisons, such as pesticides and recreational drug or heavy alcohol use, can lead to Dementia symptoms. Symptoms might resolve with treatment.
7. Brain tumors. Rarely, Dementia can result from damage caused by a brain tumor.

8. Anoxia. This condition, also called hypoxia, occurs when organ tissues aren't getting enough oxygen. Anoxia can occur due to severe sleep apneas, asthma, heart attack, carbon monoxide poisoning or other causes.

9. Normal-pressure hydrocephalus. This condition, which is caused by enlarged ventricles in the brain, can cause walking problems, urinary difficulty, and memory loss.

Risk factors

Many factors can eventually contribute to Dementia. Some factors, such as age, can't be changed. Others can be addressed to reduce your risk.

Risk factors that can't be changed

(a). Age. The risk rises as you age, especially after age 65. However, Dementia isn't a normal part of aging, and Dementia can occur in younger people.

(b). Family history. Having a family history of Dementia puts you at greater risk of developing the condition. However, many people with a family history never develop symptoms, and many people without a family history do. There are tests to determine whether you have certain genetic mutations.

(c). Down syndrome. By middle age, many people with Down syndrome develop early-onset Alzheimer's disease.

(d). Diet and exercise. Research shows that lack of exercise increases the risk of Dementia. While no specific diet is known to reduce dementia risk, research indicates a greater incidence of Dementia in people who eat unhealthy diet compared with those who follow a Mediterranean-style diet rich in produce, whole grains, nuts and seeds.

(e). Heavy alcohol use. If you drink large amounts of alcohol, you might have a higher risk of Dementia. While some studies have shown that moderate amounts of alcohol might have a protective effect, results are inconsistent. The relationship between moderate amounts of alcohol and dementia risk isn't well-understood.

(f). Cardiovascular risk factors. These include high blood pressure (hypertension), high cholesterol, a buildup of fats in your artery walls (atherosclerosis) and obesity.

(g). Depression. Although not yet well-understood, late-life depression might indicate the development of Dementia.

(h). Diabetes. Having diabetes may increase your risk of Dementia, primarily if it's poorly controlled.

(i). Smoking. Smoking might increase your risk of developing dementia and blood vessel (vascular) diseases.

(j). Sleep apnea. People who snore and have episodes where they frequently stop breathing while asleep may have reversible memory loss.

(k). Vitamin and nutritional deficiencies. Low levels of vitamin D, vitamin B-6, vitamin B-12 and folate may increase your risk of Dementia.

(l). Complications: Dementia can affect many body systems and, therefore, the ability to function. Dementia can lead to: Poor nutrition. Many people with Dementia eventually reduce or stop eating, affecting their nutrient intake. Ultimately, they may be unable to chew and swallow.

Pneumonia. Difficulty swallowing increases the risk of choking or aspirating food into the lungs, preventing breathing and causing pneumonia.

Inability to perform self-care tasks. As Dementia progresses, it can interfere with bathing, dressing, brushing hair or teeth, using the toilet independently, and taking medications accurately.

Personal safety challenges. Some day-to-day situations can present safety issues for Dementia people, including driving, cooking, and walking alone.

Death. Late-stage Dementia results in coma and death, often from an infection.

Prevention

There's no sure way to prevent Dementia, but there are steps you can take that might help. More research is needed, but it might be beneficial to do the following:

- Keep your mind active. Mentally stimulating activities, such as reading, solving puzzles and playing word games, and memory training might delay the onset of Dementia and decrease its effects.

- Be physically and socially active. Physical activity and social interaction might delay the onset of Dementia and reduce its symptoms. Move more and aim for 150 minutes of exercise a week.

- Quit smoking. Some studies have shown that smoking in middle age and beyond may increase your risk of dementia and blood vessel (vascular) conditions. Quitting smoking might reduce your risk and will improve your health.

- Get enough vitamins. Some research suggests that people with low levels of vitamin D in their blood are more likely to develop Alzheimer's disease and other forms of Dementia. You can get vitamin D through certain foods, supplements, and sun exposure. More study is needed before an increase in vitamin D intake is recommended for preventing Dementia. But, it is a good idea to make sure you get adequate vitamin D. Taking a daily B-complex vitamin, and vitamin C may also be helpful.

- Manage cardiovascular risk factors. Treat high blood pressure, high cholesterol, diabetes, and high body mass index (BMI). High blood pressure might lead to a higher risk of some types of Dementia. More research is needed to determine whether treating high blood pressure may reduce the risk of Dementia.

- Treat health conditions. See your doctor for treatment if you experience hearing loss, depression, or anxiety.

- Maintain a healthy diet. Eating a healthy diet is essential for many reasons, but a diet such as the Mediterranean diet rich in fruits, vegetables, whole grains, and omega-3 fatty acids, which are commonly found in certain fish and nuts-might promote health and lower your risk of developing Dementia. This type of diet also improves cardiovascular health, which may help lower dementia risk. Try eating fatty fish such as salmon three times a week, and a handful of nuts especially, almonds and walnuts daily.

- Get enough sleep. Practice good sleep hygiene, and talk to your doctor if you snore or have periods where you stop breathing or gasp during sleep.

Chapter 8

----·······◦◦◦◦◦◦◦·······----

The Challenges of Developmental Disability

Developmental Disability

What if you have a family member born with a diagnosis of developmental disability, what would you do?

WELFARE AND INSTITUTIONS CODE–WIC DIVISION 4.5. SERVICES FOR THE DEVELOPMENTALLY DISABLED [4500-4885] (Division 4.5 added by Stats. 1977, Ch. 1252.).CHAPTER 1.6. General Provisions [4507-4519.8](Chapter 1.6 heading added by Stats. 2014, Ch. 178, Sec. 4.) 4512. (a) "Developmental disability" means a disability that originates before an individual attains 18 years of age; continues, or can be expected to continue, indefinitely; and constitutes a substantial disability for that individual. As defined by the Director of Developmental Services, in consultation with the Superintendent of Public Instruction, this term shall include intellectual disability, cerebral palsy, epilepsy, and Autism. This term shall also include disabling conditions found to be closely related to intellectual disability or to require treatment similar to that required for individuals with an intellectual disability, but shall not include other handicapping conditions that are solely physical in nature.

(a) "Consumer" means a person who has a disability that meets the definition of developmental disability set forth in subdivision (a).
(b) "Natural supports" means personal associations and relationships typically developed in the community that enhance the quality and security of life for people, including, but not limited to,

family relationships, friendships reflecting the diversity of the neighborhood and the community, associations with fellow students or employees in regular classrooms and workplaces, and associations developed through participation in clubs, organizations, and other civic activities.

(c) "Circle of support" means a committed group of community members, who may include family members, meeting regularly with an individual with developmental disabilities in order to share experiences, promote autonomy and community involvement, and assist the individual in establishing and maintaining natural supports. A circle of support generally includes a plurality of members who neither provide nor receive services or supports for persons with developmental disabilities and who do not receive payment for participation in the circle of support.

(d) "Facilitation" means the use of modified or adapted materials, special instructions, equipment, or personal assistance by an individual, such as assistance with communications, that will enable a consumer to understand and participate to the maximum extent possible in the decisions and choices that affect his or her life.

(e) "Family support services" means services and supports that are provided to a child with developmental disabilities or his or her family and that contributes to the ability of the family to reside together.

(f) "Voucher" means any authorized alternative form of service delivery in which the consumer or family member is provided with payment, coupon, or other form of authorization that enables the consumer family member to choose his or her own service provider.

(g) "Planning team" means the individual with developmental disabilities, the parents or legally appointed guardian of a minor consumer or the legally appointed conservator of an adult consumer, the authorized representative, including those appointed pursuant to subdivision (d) of Section 4548 and subdivision (e) of Section 4705, one or more regional center representatives, including the designated regional center service coordinator pursuant to subdivision (b) of Section 4640.7, any individual, including a service provider, invited by the consumer, the parents or legally appointed guardian of a minor consumer or the legally appointed conservator of an adult consumer, or the authorized representative, including those appointed pursuant to subdivision (d) of Section 4548 and subdivision (e) of Section 4705, and including a minor's, dependent's, or ward's court-appointed developmental services decision maker appointed pursuant to Section 319, 361, or 726.

(h) "Stakeholder organizations" means statewide organizations representing the interests of consumers, family members, service providers, and statewide advocacy organizations.

(i) (1). "Substantial disability" means the existence of significant functional limitations in three or more of the following areas of major life activity, as determined by a regional center, and as appropriate to the age of the person:

(A). Self-care.
(B). Receptive and expressive language.
(C). Learning.
(D). Mobility.
(E). Self-direction.
(F). Capacity for independent living.
(G). Economic self-sufficiency.

(2). A reassessment of substantial disability for purposes of continuing eligibility shall utilize the same criteria under which the individual was originally made eligible. "Native language" means the language normally used or the preferred language identified by the individual and, when appropriate, his or her parent, legal guardian or conservator, or authorized representative.

Child's Milestone of Development as a Guide

From the time of birth of your child, as a parent, you must be on the lookout and observe for physical signs of improvement and possible changes that could impact your child's future growth and development. If you find something out of the ordinary or signs of concern such as possible developmental disability, you must immediately contact a physician or any health care professional. Developmental disabilities are a group of conditions attributed to impairment(s) in physical, learning, language, or behavior areas. These conditions begin during the developmental period, may impact day-to-day functioning, and usually last throughout a person's lifetime.

Every child from birth undergoes milestone of development that gives us a broad generalized idea as to how our child develops the much skills needed skills as he grows and matures. Skills such as taking a first step, smiling for the first time, and waving "bye-bye" are called developmental milestones. Children reach milestones in how they play, learn, speak, behave, and move (for example, crawling and walking). They develop at their own pace and it is impossible to know exactly when a child will learn a certain milestone on skill development.

As a parent, you know your child well and you can determine when your child is not meeting the milestones for his or her age, or if you observe a problem with the way your child walks, speaks, plays, learns, etc... In seeing signs that seem out of the norm, immediately consult with your physician.

Monitoring and Screening

As a parent, you must coordinate your child's growth and development with a health care professional. During visits with a physician or a healthcare professional, they monitor and evaluate your child for milestones and possible developmental delays. Any problems noticed during developmental monitoring should be followed up with a developmental screening.

Developmental screening is a short test to tell if a child is learning basic skills when he or she should, or if there are delays. Early identification and intervention can have a significant impact on a child's ability to learn new skills, as well as reduce the need for costly interventions over time.

Risk Factors Involved

Developmental disabilities begin anytime during the developmental period and usually last throughout a person's lifetime. Most developmental disabilities begin before a baby is born, but some can happen after birth because of injury, infection, or other factors. Most developmental disabilities are thought to be caused by a complex variable factors which may include genetics, parental health and behaviors (such as smoking and drinking) during pregnancy, birth complications, infections the mother might have during pregnancy or the baby might have very early in life, exposure of the mother or child to high levels of environmental toxins, like lead, mercury, etc.

For some developmental disabilities, such as fetal alcohol syndrome, we know it is one of their direct causes by drinking alcohol during pregnancy. However, there are others we do not know, as they require further research. Some of the most common known causes of intellectual disability include fetal alcohol syndrome; genetic and chromosomal conditions, such as Down syndrome and fragile X syndrome; and certain infections during pregnancy.

Children who have a sibling with Autism are at a higher risk of also having autism spectrum disorder. Low birth-weight, premature birth, multiple birth, and infections during pregnancy are associated with an increased risk for many developmental disabilities.

Untreated newborn jaundice (high levels of bilirubin in the blood during the first few days after birth) can cause a type of brain damage known as kernicterus. Children with kernicterus are more likely to have cerebral palsy, hearing and vision problems, and teeth problems. Early detection and treatment of newborn jaundice can prevent kernicterus.

Who Is Affected with Developmental Disabilities?

Developmental disabilities occur among all racial, ethnic, and socioeconomic groups. Recent estimates in the United States show that about one in six, or about 17%, of children aged 3 through 17 years have one or more developmental disabilities, such as:

- ADHD,
- autism spectrum disorder,
- cerebral palsy,
- hearing loss,
- intellectual disability
- learning disability,
- vision impairment
- and other developmental delays

Suppose you discover that a child or a loved one is diagnosed with developmental disabilities. In that case, it is incredibly beneficial that you get in contact with any Regional Center located in your county, particularly in the state of California.

Regional Centers Benefits, Resources and the Appeals Process

Regional Centers are non-profit private corporations that contract with the Department of Developmental Services to provide or coordinate services and supports for individuals with developmental disabilities. They have offices throughout California to provide a local resource to help find and access the many services available to individuals and their families.

To be eligible for services, a person must have a disability that begins before the person's 18th birthday, be expected to continue indefinitely and present a substantial disability as defined in Section 4512 of the California Welfare and Institutions Code. The disability may include by not always limited to intellectual disability, cerebral palsy, epilepsy, and Autism. This term shall also include disabling conditions found to be closely related to intellectual disability or to require treatment similar to that required for individuals with an intellectual disability, but shall not include other handicapping conditions that are solely physical in nature. Eligibility is established through diagnosis and assessment performed by any regional center in your area of residence. Infants and toddlers (age 0 to 36 months) who are at risk of having developmental disabilities or who have a developmental delay may also qualify for services. The criteria for determining the eligibility of infants and toddlers is specified in Section 95014 of the California Government Code. In addition, individuals at risk of having a child with a developmental disability may be eligible for genetic diagnosis, counseling and other prevention services provided by Early Start.

Services Provided By Regional Centers

When you have doubts whether your child or an adult member of you family (even if they already have previous diagnosis of a developmental disability), the very first step upon establishing you residency in California is to go to the closest Regional Center in your area. Regardless of their immigration or residency status in the United States, they may be able to receive the mandated services, possibly including assistance in adjustments in immigration status. A family member who has no legal immigration background may be referred to the local immigration assistance services such as the Catholic Charities and Advocacy groups that may help.

When I was a Case Manager at one of the Regional Centers in the early 1990's, I had the opportunity of assisting several foreign nationals, and their families with developmental disabilities acquire temporary immigration relief and regional center services that they are entitled under The Act. In order to accomplish this, however, one must bring every available documentation, pictures, government-issued certifications etc… that could be helpful in the process. It will be a long and difficult challenge, but with patience and perseverance, it can be achieved.

There are 21 Regional Centers established under the Lanterman Act to serve your family's needs. Regional Centers provide diagnosis and assessment of eligibility and help plan, access, coordinate and monitor the services and supports that are needed because of a developmental disability. There is no charge for the diagnosis and eligibility assessment.

Once eligibility is determined, a case manager or service coordinator is assigned to help develop a plan for services, tell you where services are available, and help you get the services. Most services and supports are free regardless of age or income.

There is a requirement for parents to share the cost of 24-hour out-of-home placements for children under age 18. This share depends on the parents' ability to pay. There may also be a co-payment requirement for other selected services.

Some of the services and supports provided by the regional centers include:

1. Information and referral
2. Assessment and diagnosis
3. Counseling
4. Lifelong individualized planning and service coordination

5. Purchase of necessary services included in the individual program plan
6. Resource development
7. Outreach
8. Assistance in finding and using community and other resources
9. Advocacy for the protection of legal, civil and service right.
10. Early intervention services for at risk infants and their families
11. Genetic counseling
12. Family support
13. Planning, placement, and monitoring for 24-hour out-of-home care
14. Training and educational opportunities for individuals and families
15. Community education about developmental disabilities

Regional centers provide a wide array of services for individuals with developmental disabilities. Each center provides diagnosis and assessment of eligibility, and helps plan, access, coordinate and monitor services and supports. Once eligibility is determined, most services and supports are free regardless of age or income; however, there are a few exceptions. For example, the Parental Fee Program requires that the parent(s) of a minor receiving 24-hour out-of-home residential services be assessed a fee for services.

In making decisions about services needed, the planning team, which includes the person using the services, family members, regional center staff, and others who may be asked to attend the planning meeting by the individual, will join together to discuss the supports needed that are related to the developmental disability.

Generic resources are the services that are provided by other agencies that have a legal responsibility to fund them. State law says that regional centers cannot pay for services for which another agency has responsibility. Examples of "Generic Resources" include:

- California Children's Services
- City, County, and State Housing Services

- Community Legal Services
- County Medical Clinics
- County Mental Health and/or Behavioral Health Services
- Department of Rehabilitation
- Education System (Private and/or Public)
- Family Resource Centers
- Health Care Insurance (Private and/or Public)
- In-Home Supportive Services

It is also important to know that the state also has a unique program known as the Self-Determination Program, which provides children and adult consumers freedom, control, and responsibility in choosing other services and supports to help meet their needs.

It is your right to Appeal

The state's developmental services community is best served by an open exchange of information and opinions, and DDS is committed to resolving problems and concerns when they occur. Below are the multiple options consumers, family members, vendors and providers have for filing appeals and complaints.

This process is a mechanism to be used when an individual consumer, or any representative acting on behalf of a consumer, believes that any right has been wrongly or unfairly denied by a regional center, developmental center, or a service provider. This process is not to be used by consumers to resolve disputes about eligibility, or the nature, scope, or amount of services.

Fair Hearing

The fair hearing process is for resolving disputes with a regional or developmental center about eligibility or the nature, scope, or amount of services and supports.

As a sample story, my brother has a son and his name is Michael (not real name) who was born in a foreign country. Michael was born with a diagnosis of Autism. Michael was petitioned as a green card holder when he came

103

to the United States at the age of 15. Michael had behavior and learning disability related to his diagnosis prior to and upon arriving in California. Michael and his dad applied for Regional Center support and assistance but were denied services at least twice because he was deemed as not having the diagnosis that makes him eligible for Regional Center services. Michael was seen by a couple of physicians in California who confirm that he has diagnosis of Autism. The family even went on to secure hospital records and physician notes from his birth place that indicated and supported his diagnosis. Michael's family requested for an appeal twice from the Director of Regional Center of the service area in the county where they live that denied the services until they requested the intervention from the Area Board and the Fair Hearings Board who advocated for his rights under the Act. After several months of documents presentation and discussion, Michael finally acquired his disability benefits under the Lanterman Act.

Although the effort resulted into a positive outcome which was the approval of his services, in the event that his services were denied, my brother may once again appeal the final decision of the hearings. The final step in this process is for my brother to file civil lawsuit in the County Superior Court to challenge the regional center decision because they know that their son has the diagnosis and shall severely suffer and will be impacted if he does not receive the services he is entitled to under the Lanterman Act. In conclusion, my nephew's request for services was granted by the Court under the Act. The bottom line is that Regional Centers are mere overseer of State and Federal Funds allocated for individuals with developmental disabilities. If an individual is born with the disability or acquires the disability defined under the Act before he reaches 18 years old, Regional Centers are mandated to provide the required services established under the Lanterman Act.

Early Start Complaint Processes

Early Start is for infants and toddlers under the age of three who are at risk of having a developmental disability or have a developmental disability or delay, and their families. There are three separate processes in place for addressing disagreements which arise under this program. This is a voluntary process, on the part of both parties, to resolve disagreements between a parent and a regional center or a local educational agency involving any matter related to Early Start or related to a proposal or refusal to change or initiate the identification, evaluation, assessment, placement, or services. Mediation may be used as a first option for resolution or may be requested at any time during a due process hearing or the compliant process. The mediation conference must be completed within 30 days from the receipt of the request by the Office of Administrative Law.

The process is used to resolve disagreements between parents and a regional center or local educational agency involving any matter related to Early Start or related to a proposal or refusal to change or initiate the identification, evaluation, assessment, placement, or services. This hearing must be completed within 30 days from receipt of the request by the Office of Administrative Law. The decision is final unless appealed to the Superior Court of appropriate jurisdiction or civil action is brought by any aggrieved parties.

The process is used to investigate and resolve any alleged violation of federal or state statutes or regulations governing the Early Start program. DDS, and if the complaint involves a local educational agency, the California Department of Education, investigates the allegations and issues a written decision to all parties within 60 days of receipt of the complaint. (See California Code of Regulations, Title 17, Sections 52170-52174)

Title 17 Complaint Procedures

This procedure is to be used when: (1) one of the "personal rights" of an individual who resides in a developmental center, community care or health care facility, has been formally denied by the facility as allowed in Title 17 of California Code of Regulation Section 50530; and (2) the consumer disagrees with the facility's decision.

Chapter 9

Medicaid, Medicare Benefits and Insurance Coverage

Cost of Surgery and Hospitalization

In the event that you or a loved one needed to be hospitalized due to pre-existing condition, chemo-therapy, illness or injury caused by an accident, here are some brief ideas that could help ease up on the stress of hospitalization. Depending on the reason for hospitalization, (in my case it was cervical stenosis which is a surgery on the spine in my neck) it can be very stressful physically, emotionally and financially. It is particularly stressful for a child, an elderly or an individual with cognitive and physical challenges due to the level and degree of understanding the complexity and impact of the hospitalization. This is when our role as a caregiver is very important to advocate for our loved one, speak and act for their benefit however, the care receiver has the final decision. There is also the high level of stress in figuring out what to do before, during and after the hospitalization, the cost of the procedure, hospitalization and the continuum of care which most people can not afford without any insurance coverage and a deeper bank account. No worries because in this chapter, we will learn a little bit about how we can afford the procedure without having so much stress. For now, we need to have an idea about the average cost of a surgical procedure.

How much does an average surgery and hospitalization cost?

In the United States, data shows hospital cost are at a staggering $384.5 billion a year. The average hospital stay costs over $10,000 per day but the amount varies widely depending on the medical condition that you have. Survey shows that there are 35 most expensive medical conditions that account for more than 70% of all hospital costs. During most hospitalizations, typically Medicare cover 46% of that cost, Medicaid pay for 17%. Private insurance pay for 28%, while 9% out of pocket from insured patients. For those who are uninsured or does not have Medicare-Medicaid or private insurance coverage, cost is mostly done out of pocket. Besides the hospitalization cost, there is the surgical procedure, transportation and post-operation therapy. Just to have a general idea of hospitalization cost estimates are indicated but they appear to be very costly which explains why surgery is the ultimate option that most people refuse to consider. The average cost is also based on the number of hospital stay and the estimates vary on location, the hospital and other factors. The average cost of common surgeries and hospitalization guesstimates in 2018:

- heart valve replacement: $170,000,
- heart bypass: $123,000
- spinal fusion: $110,000
- hip replacement: $40,364
- knee replacement: $35,000
- angioplasty: $28,2000
- hip resurfacing: $28,000
- gastric bypass: $25,000
- cornea: $17,500
- gastric sleeve: $16,000

These are just the estimated cost for surgery but there are numerous potential "add-on" costs to the surgery that are not included until after the whole procedure is thoroughly discussed in detail, then it really becomes stressful.

Now let us review the cost for hospitalization:

- Pancreatic disorders: Average cost per stay: $9,727
- Pneumonia: a lung condition caused by an infectious inflammation of the air sacs: Average cost per stay: $9,793.
- Diabetes mellitus with complications: Conditions that occur from poor treatment of diabetes are wide-ranging, from vascular diseases, blindness, and chronic kidney disease: Average cost per stay: $9,850
- Diverticulosis and diverticulitis: Diverticulosis is the presence of bulging pouches in the digestive track and diverticulitis occurs when the pouches become inflamed or infected.: Average cost per stay: $10,169
- Cardiac dysrhythmias: a medical term for an irregular heartbeat. Average cost per stay: $10,191.
- Intestinal obstruction without hernia: A food or liquid blockage that may be caused by Crohn's Disease, colon cancer, or other diseases. Average cost per stay: $10,944
- Congestive heart failure: is the inability to pump an adequate amount of blood through the body and can be caused by many diseases. Average cost per stay: $11,500
- Other nervous system disorders: Trauma, infections, and tumors are some of the many conditions that afflict the brain, spine, nerves, eyes, ears, or other parts of the nervous system. Average cost per stay: $11,538
- Other gastrointestinal disorders: Food allergies, lactose intolerance, and celiac disease are some of the many disorders that harm functionality of the stomach and intestines. Average cost per stay: $11,564
- Pulmonary heart disease: A high blood pressure that affects lung arteries and the right side of your heart results in pulmonary hypertension. Average cost per stay: $11,564

- Biliary tract disease: Biliary diseases are a group of conditions that affect the biliary system---including gallstones and pancreatitis. Average cost per stay: $11,764
- Hypertension with complications and secondary hypertension: Unlike pulmonary hypertension (heart disease), secondary hypertension is high blood pressure caused by another medical condition: Average cost per stay: $12,164.
- Other nutritional, endocrine, and metabolic disorders: Osteoporosis, cystic fibrosis, and obesity are major diseases related to glands and metabolism. Average cost per stay: $12,173
- Complications of surgical procedures or medical care: Any side effect of surgery or a basic medical procedure is included here. Average cost per stay: $13,565
- Rehabilitation care, fitting of prostheses, and adjustment of rehabilitation and therapeutic devices: Rehabilitation includes "services that help you keep, get back, or improve skills and functioning for daily living that have been lost or impaired because you were sick, hurt, or disabled. Average cost per stay: $13,877
- Other fractures: This category includes broken bones that are not in their own category such as skull breaks. Average cost per stay: $14,149.
- Abdominal hernia: A protrusion of an organ through tissue and often occurs by the pelvic floor or abdominal wall. Average cost per stay: $14,447
- Acute cerebrovascular disease: Cerebrovascular disease impacts the blood flow in the brain and often results in strokes. Average cost per stay $15,378
- Osteoarthritis: A degenerative joint disease causes the wearing down of tissue between joints. Average cost per stay: $15,897
- Maintenance chemotherapy, radiotherapy: Chemo and radiation therapy are both types of cancer treatment. Average cost per stay: $15,988

- Fracture of neck of femur (hip): Breaks in the neck of the femur are common among athletes and elderly individuals with osteoporosis. Average cost per stay: $16,133.
- Peripheral and visceral atherosclerosis: Atherosclerosis restricts blood flow to the heart by clogging of the inner walls of the arteries. Average cost per stay: $16,771
- Fracture of lower limb: Broken hips, knees, tibias, ankles, and other lower body bones are included here. Average cost per stay: $16,796
- Secondary malignancies: New cancers that arrive as a result of treatment of a first cancer are described as secondary malignancies. Average cost per stay: $17,163
- Cancer of bronchus, lung: Lung cancer or bronchial carcinoma: is mainly caused by smoking. Average cost per stay: $17,530
- Respiratory failure, insufficiency, arrest (adult): Respiratory failure and insufficiency happens when the lungs cannot produce enough oxygen or expel enough carbon dioxide. Respiratory arrest is the cessation of breathing. Average cost per stay: $17,868
- Septicemia: or sepsis is blood poisoning caused by a bacterial infection. Average cost per stay: $18,031
- Spondylosis, intervertebral disc disorders, other back problems: Spondylosis refers to any degeneration of the spine. Invertebral disc disorders is the breakdown of the discs in between the bones of the spine. Average cost per stay: $18,978.

Why is it so expensive?

Surgery and hospitalization cost estimates are terribly expensive and may appear to be unaffordable to everyone. However, our goal is to understand why the cost is staggering and we will learn how to deal with it by finding out various ways to afford it in order to help us deal with our pain and stress.

First let us understand why the cost is so high. Depending on the state and county where you live, cost does vary. While some procedures are less expensive than others, none are cheap and some cost hundreds of thousands of dollars because there are many additional costs associated with surgery that not specified on the pre-operation conference that are not so obvious but forms part of the whole procedure. Surgical fees that are billed by the hospital are often very different from what is actually paid by insurance, Medicare, and Medicaid. Insurers often negotiate significant discounts on services provided. If you are paying for surgery out of pocket, be sure to ask for the rate that insurance companies pay. You are also entitled to an itemized bill that lists each expense and unspecified fees of the estimated costs that forms part of your final bill.

What are the unspecified fees that form part of the estimated cost?

1. Physician Fees: The vast majority of surgeries require at least two or more physicians. There is always at least one surgeon performing the procedure, and an anesthesiologist. For more involved surgeries, several surgeons may work together to perform the surgery. Each physician involved in the procedure will usually submit a bill for their services.

2. Additional Staff in the Operating Room: In addition to the physicians participating in the surgery, there are at least two additional staff members in the operating room during the procedure. A circulating nurse is present, charting everything that happens during the procedure and doing the things that the "scrubbed in" staff cannot.

3. A surgical technologist, commonly known as a Surg Tech, or ST, is the person responsible for handing the surgeon the sterile instruments used during the procedure. The fee for this staff may be included in the operating room fee.

4. The Operating Room: An operating room is billed in 15-minute increments in most facilities. The fees include the

sterilization and use of instruments, the anesthesia machinery, the cleaning of the room after the procedure, and other items that are used during the surgery.

5. Surgical Implants: If your surgery requires an implant, such as an artificial hip or a mesh graft, there will be a fee for the implant. The price of implants varies widely, but the fact that they have to be sterile, made to perform for a lifetime and require extensive research and testing usually makes them quite costly.

6. Medications: The medications used during surgery are an additional expense during surgery. The medications given range from IV fluids and anesthesia medications to any special drugs that are necessary during the procedure such as an antibiotic.

7. Recovery Room: The recovery room often referred to as the Post Anesthesia Care Unit or PACU, is where patients are taken after surgery to be monitored while the anesthesia wears off completely. There may be an individual charge for the time spent in recovery, along with any medications given.

8. Pre-Surgery Testing and Care: Your road to surgery will begin with a consultation with your surgeon, which will result in a fee. Any additional visits with your surgeon, both before and after surgery, may also result in fees. The surgeon may order testing additional to make sure you are healthy enough to tolerate the stresses of surgery. These tests may range from blood tests and chest x-rays to stress tests, imaging tests (CT, MRI, Ultrasound, PET scans) and any additional tests that the surgeon deems necessary. These tests can range from hundreds of dollars to thousands of dollars each and can add substantially to the cost of surgery.

    The day of your surgery may also result in additional fees for pre-operative procedures (such as inserting an IV) and standard blood work.

9. Hospital Care: If the recovery from surgery is done on an inpatient basis, there will be a substantial fee for the hospital room and the nursing care that accompanies it. At this time, additional tests, medications or care may be required, all of which will increase the cost of the procedure. If your recovery takes place in the ICU, as is common with open heart surgery, transplants, major lung surgery, and trauma, you can expect the cost to rise significantly. In some cities, 24 hours in an ICU costs a minimum of $5,000 not including standard ICU care such as x-rays, blood tests, and medications.

10. Consultation by Physicians: When the surgeons and any other physicians who are participating in your care check in on you each day during your recovery, an additional fee is often generated. This is how the doctors are paid for their time and expertise when you are being cared for in the hospital.

11. Physical and Occupational Therapy: After some surgeries, such as orthopedic surgery, physical therapy is often part of the recovery process. Physical and occupational therapists will assist you in getting back on your feet as quickly as possible and returning to your normal activity.

12. Social Workers: Social workers are an important part of coping with a hospitalization for many people. Social workers help people determine ways to pay for a surgery (for example, social workers would help you apply for government benefits) they also help plan your discharge from the hospital. If you need a special bed at home, or if you need to spend some time at a rehabilitation facility before returning home, social workers help make those arrangements. There is usually no individual fee for social work.

Miscellaneous Additions: If you require crutches, a cane or a similar appliance before your discharge, you will probably see it on your bill. The same is true for products like supportive stockings to prevent blood clots, binders to support an incision, or a sling to support an arm in a cast etc...

How are you going to pay for all these cost?

Surgical procedure and hospitalization cost can be very expensive that is why majority of patients refuse to undertake for obvious reasons, However, do not be afraid as there are several ways to make the surgery happen. Read on through the succeeding chapters as the book tackles on the important subject to finance the surgical procedure at an affordable cost or sometimes for free.

There are several ways to pay for surgery such as Medicare, Medicaid. Private pay, etc. which will be discussed in this chapter.

As a common practice in most states, Private Health Insurance (HMO) (PPO) pays for approximately 34% of all hospital care. Out-of-pocket costs comprise 11% of the total, while 18% are covered by other sources, including all other public health insurance programs, such as the Children's Health Insurance Program (CHIP), and programs of the Department of Veterans Affairs (VA) and the Department of Defense (DOD); and other third-party payers, including workers' compensation, and other state and local programs. Patients may have to pay co-pays, deductibles or the total cost of hospital care and surgery.

The best-case scenario is for the patient to have primary insurance such as Kaiser, Blue Cross etc. to pay for most of the expenses, along with a secondary form of insurance like Aflac, Care, or SCAN that pays the remaining expenses. But even if you have excellent insurance coverage that pays 80% of the total bill, the remaining 20% can exceed $100,000 for major surgery. Sometimes, in the case of self-employed individual, private insurance can be obtained outside of the workplace. It could cover a big portion of the surgery cost, but most insurance plans have a "cap" or maximum that the company will pay. In some major surgeries, that cap is met or exceeded by standard care during the procedure. If you are not fortunate enough to afford private insurance coverage, there is financial assistance you can avail to cover hospitalization, surgery and medication through the federal and state funded insurance programs known as Medicaid and Medicare.

Medicaid (MediCal) and Medicare

Medicare and **Medi-Cal** are respectively recognized as federal and state funded health coverage for American citizens, but they do so in different

Romwell M. Sabeniano, MBA.HCM

ways for different demographics. Medicare provides federal health coverage to individuals 65 and older or those with a severe disability regardless of income, whereas Medi-Cal (California's state-run and funded Medicaid program) provides health coverage to those families with very low income, as well as pregnant women and the blind, among others. Coverage is not mutually exclusive: individuals who are eligible for both programs may receive dual coverage.

Medicare was signed into law by President Johnson in 1965 as a federal health insurance program designed to assist Americans over the age of 65 pay for their medical costs. Since then, Medicare has expanded significantly to cover more services and provide coverage to more people, including young people who are eligible for Social Security Disability benefits and those individuals suffering from end-stage renal disease. Medicare is now divided into four distinct parts, with each providing different coverage types and packages:

- **Medicare Part A**: Includes coverage for inpatient hospital and nursing facility, stays, as well as hospice and some in-home healthcare. Premiums for Part A are mostly covered by payroll deductions while the individual was employed.
- **Medicare Part B:** Includes coverage for doctor visits (including preventive services), medical supplies, and outpatient care. There does exist a monthly contribution, although this is usually expensed as a deduction in social security payments. (Taken together, Medicare Parts A and B are usually referred to as "Traditional Medicare" or "Original Medicare.").
- **Medicare Part C:** Also referred to as a "Medicare Advantage Plan," Part C is an alternative insurance plan offered by private insurers that provides Traditional Medicare and prescription drug coverage under a single policy.
- **Medicare Part D:** Part D was added as a Medicare option in 2003 and provides prescription drug coverage for those who have Original Medicare, some Medicare Cost Plans, some Medicare Private-Fee-for-Service Plans, and Medicare Medical Savings Account Plans. This plan is available for

purchase through private companies, and premiums are subsidized by the federal government.

Medi-Cal provides health coverage to low-income individuals and families for free or at significantly lower cost than those plans offered through Covered California. Like all plans offered through the Health Exchange, Medi-Cal plans are required to offer certain "essential health benefits," such as emergency services, hospitalization, mental health services, and addiction treatment. Those individuals and families whose household income is equal to or more than 138% of the poverty line are eligible to receive health benefits through Medi-Cal. Additionally, individuals can also receive Medi-Cal if any of the following items apply to them:

- Over the age of 65,
- Blind,
- Disabled, * Under 21,
- Pregnant,
- Live in a nursing or intermediate care facility,
- Have received limited refugee status, depending on how long the individual has been in the United States,
- Have received breast and/or cervical cancer screening.

Individuals enrolled in any of the following programs are also eligible to receive health benefits through Medi-Cal:

- Cal Fresh
- SSI/SSP
- CalWorks (AFDC)
- Refugee Assistance
- Foster Care or Adoption Assistance Program

Eligible individuals can apply online at CoveredCA.com to determine if they qualify. They can also apply at their local county human services agency or by calling (800) 300-1516. Those individuals who qualify will receive a benefits identification card (BIC) to begin using in order to receive healthcare services. Medi-Cal participants will also receive a packet detailing 21 available health plans for them to choose from, although options will vary depending on the county in which you and your family reside. However, each county's Medi-Cal plans provide high quality care at little or no cost, regardless of where you live. With more than 400 hospitals and 13,000 doctors, dentists, pharmacists, and other participating medical providers, your client or family member should have no problem finding the best healthcare fit for their unique needs.

No Insurance, No Problem. There are creative ways to have surgery

Yes you can still have your much needed surgery. Even if you are unemployed, do not have private insurance, a foreigner or undocumented alien, you can still, for emergency purpose can have your surgery and hospitalization that you need. There are numerous creative ways to cover the costs of surgery such as self-pay, borrowing from Retirement Benefits, etc.. Veterans Benefits, Medicare, Medicaid etc.. Even if you do not have insurance, here are more recommendations for you to consider:

- **Prevention:** Stay healthy, eat healthy and exercise daily. "Prevention is the key to health. Stop smoking, avoid alcohol and fatty diet. If you can, utilize the public care clinics and consult with a doctor and follow their recommendations to keep yourself healthy.
- **Reduce Surgery Costs:** Negotiate: Research for a city, county or state where it cost less for the procedure from anesthesia to the surgeon to the hospital and the pharmacy. Call everyone who is providing the care and explain your particular situation. Request for the best rate in services that are offered to insurance companies. Persistence plays a role together with a request in a pleasant manner while seeking discounts or cost reduction which can be in thousands of dollars off your bill. People in billing will often help, whether it's pointing

you toward programs for people with financial difficulties or providing inside information. Use the surgery center instead of a hospital. In order to be able to negotiate, ask yourself these questions: questions you should ask: How long will you have to repay the loan? How much are the payments? Will you be able to manage the payments? Or will you struggle to pay your bills on time? Will the payments put too much stress on your credit cards because you can't pay more than the minimum? What's the strategy if the cost of surgery becomes higher than the original estimation?

- **Surgery in Other countries:** If local surgery is too expensive, there are identical services or procedures being offered at a lower cost or even free in some other countries which one can search on-line. Due to the ever-increasing and unaffordable cost of healthcare in the United States, there is a common practice known as "medical tourism". In some cases, the same procedures may cost 75% less than in the US. Sometimes, foreign surgeons promote and advertise themselves masked as clinical trials for a new trend in surgical procedure which oftentimes at no cost to the patient. But be beware that sometimes you get for what you pay. I would do some research on the credibility of the hospital surgeon and the facility where the surgery will take place before you decide on this.

- **Temporary Disability:** There are some procedures that qualify for state disability which one may apply. Look on line at the MediCaid and Medicare website, perhaps your disability might qualify for benefits. This short-term benefit may not pay for the surgery itself, but it could provide financial help during your time of recovery. There are limits on the monthly benefits and the length of time when you can receive them.

- **Government-offered Programs:** There are programs in the local community that offers financial assistance such as Insure Kids Now offered to low-income working parents who don't have health insurance (or whose insurance doesn't cover their kids). The Children's Health Insurance Program (CHIP) provides free or low-cost health insurance for kids.

- **Veteran's Benefits:** There are some veterans who are eligible for free healthcare without copays through the U.S. Department of Veterans Affairs (VA). Seniors (65 and over) can get surgical coverage through Medicare. Some states offer medical coverage for those with low income. If you're facing major surgery, you might qualify, even if you haven't applied in the past.

- **Telemedicine:** Video conference: With the advanced technology and to keep the cost down, doctor is able to consult with a patient via video conferencing without leaving home or place, and it can help alleviate the need for a patient to stay in a hospital which can be expensive. Doctor consultations done on a per-call basis can be ideal for people who don't have insurance because they are so much less expensive than an in-person visit.

- **Payment Plans:** There are commonly Offered payment plan for surgeries that are routinely paid for by the patient instead of an insurance company. It is a formal agreement for arranging affordable monthly payments which is in a form of a credit or a loan that involves the patient and the hospital or surgeon. This approach may be very important in the case of an unplanned or emergency surgery, hospitals are usually happy to establish a payment plan with willing patients. Monthly payments are more attractive than NO PAYMENTS at all. Never ignore calls from the hospital's collection department.

- **Medical Crowd-funding:** This has become a routine process in recent years, such as a GoFundMe that is powered by donors and it's particularly effective for medical needs. You can start a campaign or one can be started for you by appealing to the general public. This approach is quite interesting because there are literally millions of people and international companies around the world that has tons of money that they can donate and declare such goodwill gesture in a form of a tax write-off at the end of the fiscal year. You will be surprised when you try this approach.

- **The Nest Egg:** Spending your life savings on surgery is definitely not ideal. But if the surgery improves your quality of life, it could be money well spent.

- **Home Equity Loans:** Home-equity loans are borrowed against the value of your home that is greater than the balance of your mortgage. If your home is worth $200,000, but you owe only $150,000 to the bank, you could borrow against the $50,000 in equity. It's usually easier to obtain this type of loan instead of an unsecured loan because your house is your collateral. But be careful. If you can't make the loan payments, it could lead to foreclosure and eviction from your home.

- **Unsecured Loans:** These are loans that are not secured with any property you own. It is based on your credit and income such as a credit card and doesn't use collateral. Surgeons might have their own loan programs, but the bottom line is the interest rate. If you can obtain a more favorable rate, go for it.

- **Pawn Shop:** If you have household goods that have value such as inherited paintings, classic cars etc. pawn or sell them.

- **Clinical Trials:** Ask the doctor or the hospital if they offer procedure or surgery in exchange for clinical research or trial on groundbreaking methodology or procedure as discount if available.

- **Ask Around:** Hospitals and doctors charge different rates. If you're not tied down to a network, it pays to comparison shop, just like you would do at a store. Ask for Reduced Rates (Or Pay in Advance). Many people might be hesitant to try this, but why not? There are discounts available, but you must ask for them.

You can also pay what you can. Even a $50 monthly payment toward a hospital bill is an effort accepted in good faith.

- **Charity:** In other states and counties, there are non-profit organizations such as Catholic Charity that provides assistance in funding, immigration etc.. There are some hospitals that provide research and innovation or procedure testing for the purpose of improving or testing a service or technique in return for a free surgery or hospitalization. Pediatric cancer patients can seek treatment at St. Jude's Children's Hospital, where all treatment is free to the patient. Meanwhile, Shriner's Children's Hospitals offer free services for pediatric orthopedic patients. Nonprofits and other organizations also provide financial help for cancer patients.

- **Social Media Appeal:** Try to contact your local newspapers and TV stations to get the word out. There are Good Samaritans still among us and a medical expert may offer assistance to a patient at no cost. Tell your story because someone else is also living a parallel situation.

- **Emergency:** In the event that a person was accepted in a emergency room for urgent cases, accidents, emergency, etc... the hospital can not turn away a patient and leave them at the curb or the entrance. For humanitarian reason, hospital must provide care to individual on emergency cases. Based on my interview with several patients such as the homeless, undocumented aliens, pregnant mothers, victims of crimes and accidents, regardless of their financial status were provided care and services by the hospitals on an emergency basis and admitted at the nursing home for continuum of care. In my experience, some patients were applied by the hospital for emergency MediCal and Medicare to provide the much needed medical services to save a person's life.

Understand your medical condition and research what you need to do.

To understand my medical condition, I started researching on the Internet. In my case, my medical issue started out with a simple tingling feeling on all of my fingertips and my arms with radiating minor pain that shoots from my back all the way to my legs and feet. Initially, I ignored the signs and dismissed it as a minor discomfort. A couple of months later, during my annual physical check up, my physician recommended a complete evaluation with blood test, X-ray and MRI (Magnetic resonance imaging. MRI uses a large magnet and micro-waves technology to look at organs and structures inside the human body.

Do your research

We need to know exactly what is the medical diagnosis that is attributed to the condition. Every medical condition is unique and most of the times do not show any sign nor pain that can come along with the diagnosis. Based on the physical exam that I went through, I was diagnosed with Cervical Stenosis which is the narrowing of the nerve canal caused by calcium build up that restricts the flow of the nerves to the rest of my body. Immediately I felt scared, depressed and upset not knowing exactly what it meant. So, the second step I did was gather up my information from the research and compared it with my lab result, X-Ray and MRI including my physician notes. I went through YouTube on the surgical procedure required, analyzed the length of time of the procedure, the process of preparation for pre-Operation and post-operation, and recovery. I called my insurance and inquired if it covers the procedure and what was my share of cost.

It is best to be prepared a few days prior to the procedure. In most cases where it requires surgery, one needs to make arrangements for a caregiver, a transportation provider when getting to and from the hospital; and to make a list of what to prepare. Make sure you give your family and friends plenty of notice about your operation so they can take time-off from work to be with you, if necessary. Check your hospital's policy on visiting times and let your family and friends know.

Pre-operative assessment

As a patient, you will be asked several pertinent questions about your health, medical history, and home circumstances. If the assessment involves a visit to the hospital, some tests may be carried out to check if you have any medical problems that might need to be treated before your operation, or if you'll need special care during or after the surgery. The tests required may depend on what type of operation and the kind of anesthetic to be applied. The tests might include blood tests, urine tests, and pregnancy tests for women. The assessment will usually happen one or more days before the operation. Make sure you get the results of any previous tests and make a list of all the medications, vitamins and herbal supplements you regularly take. You will be advised on whether you need to stop eating and drinking hours before your operation. It would help if you stop taking your usual medications before going to the hospital. If your doctor has instructed you not to eat (fasting) before the operation, you must not eat or drink anything, including light snacks, sweets, and water. You need an empty stomach during surgery so you won't vomit while you're under anesthetic. If you take insulin because of diabetes, you still need to avoid eating and drinking before surgery, but make sure your medical team is aware of your condition so appropriate precautions can be taken. Remove all jewelry, body piercings, make-up, and nail polish before your operation as it can help reduce unwanted bacteria during the surgery. It also helps doctors to see your skin and nails to make sure your blood circulation is healthy.

What to pack for the hospital

If you're staying in the hospital, you may wish to pack: *nightdress or pajamas *day clothes *clean underwear *dressing gown and slippers *small hand towel *toiletries – soap, toothbrush, toothpaste, shampoo, deodorant *sanitary towels or tampons *razor and shaving materials*comb or hairbrush *book or magazines *small amount of money *medication you normally take, *and a list of the doses for each medicine *glasses or contact lenses with case *notebook and pen *healthy snacks *address book and important phone numbers, including your GP's contact details…You may want to check with your hospital about their policy on the use of mobile phones, MP3 players or tablets during your hospital stay.

The Hospitalization

After deciding that you are going to have this surgery, you or a caregiver need to know what usually takes place during the hospitalization process, and here are some necessary steps to consider:

As a caregiver, you need to know how to get your loved one to the hospital and back home for the surgery. If you are the patient, you won't be able to drive yourself home, so you should arrange transport or ask a friend or relative to help. In some cases, the hospital may arrange transport either private Ridez NEMT, Uber, Lyft, etc... Some hospitals charge for parking. Check whether you have to pay for parking at your chosen hospital. Caregiver needs to know her personal schedule to arrange accommodations for the patient's hospital appointment. If the patient is unable to meet the scheduled appointment, let the hospital know as soon as possible. Hospital staff will be able to reschedule the appointment. As the responsible party and caregiver, let the surgeon know a few days before surgery if the care-receiver develops a simple fever or cold that could cause complications. Patient will be advised whether the operation can go ahead as planned.

Admission:

The caregiver's role starts to get complicated starting from admissions to the hospital. Bring patient's admission letter which reflects the date and time of the procedure, and what time required to arrive at the hospital. The letter should also indicate which ward or department the patient should be, the hospital or ward's contact number, and the name of the consultant who'll be taking assisting the patient. When the patient arrives, he will be welcomed by a staff member, who will explain the processes to you as the caregiver and the patient. The patient will be given an identity bracelet to wear during the hospital stay. This is routine and ensures that correct information about you is checked and available at each treatment stage.

As a caregiver you need to remind the patient to take any medications that the doctor prescribed before the surgery. But if the patient normally take tablets or insulin for diabetes, as the caregiver you need to make sure you discuss this with the specialist as soon as possible before the operation. You will be asked whether the patient is allergic to any medication or antibiotic, any sensitivity to any anesthetics so precautions can be taken.

As the caregiver, family or friends can usually stay with the patient until the procedure is done, at which point you can wait in the waiting room. Check hospital's policy on visiting times. On the first few hours in the hospital, the patient will be required to undergo various procedures, and testing so patience is important. There will be several health care professionals that will be interviewing the patient in order to move forward with the process. Be prepared to show the patient's identification, social security or insurance cards, including a Power of Attorney, particularly when checking in a loved one whom you represent. If medical history is already established, the process is easier. A nurse will check for vital signs, blood pressure, heart rate, temperature, respiratory rate and oxygenation, height and weight checked. A physical assessment including listening to the patient's heart and lungs with a stethoscope, touching the patient's arms and legs to ensure he has strong pulses, looking at his eyes, ears and mouth with a bright light, ask simple questions to ensure memory is intact and ask questions about the patient's eating and bathroom habits

After health history and physical assessment is completed, the nurse may place a peripheral IV. An IV is placed if there is a need for intravenous medication such as fluid for dehydration, nausea management if patient is throwing up, or pain medication. There may also be more tests to be done, including a chest x-ray, collection of urine samples, blood work or a CT scan. An order for other tests based on any reason that the hospital may require.

The Hospital Room

Hospital rooms will include basic necessities for daily living and not much more. There is a private or semi-private room. In a semi-private room, patient will have a roommate. Ask the nurse or nursing assistant to orient you and the patient about the room, where the call bell is located in case the patient needs assistance. You may also want to know how to work the television, use the bed if it is adjustable, control the temperature in the room, use the room phone, and how the shower works.

Most hospital floors have a pantry with water, juice, and snacks available to patients. There may be a family waiting room. You can also request a map of the hospital campus including the gift shop, cafeteria, chapel and parking facilities to make available to those who would like to visit. Visiting hours vary and each hospital has policies regarding overnight guests.

After surgery

After surgery, the patient will be moved back to the ward (after local anesthetic) or a recovery room (after general anesthetic or epidural), where you as the caregiver will be updated as how the operation went. Patient may feel hazy or groggy from the general anesthetic. A nurse may give oxygen (through tubes in to the nose or a mask) to help patient feel better. It is common to feel sick or vomit after being given general anesthesia. A nurse may offer medicine to help with sickness. Patient may also have a sore throat and dry mouth. Blood pressure will be taken regularly. This will either be done by a nurse or by using an automatic cuff that squeezes tightly at regular times. Temperature will also be taken.

Coping with pain and recovery

Patient will have some pain after surgery. Tell the nurse as soon as patient start to feel any pain so they can give patient with pain reducing medication as soon as possible. Pain medication can take effect within 20 minutes or less.

The sooner the patient starts to move around, the better. Lying in bed for too long can cause blood to pool in the legs possibly lead to at risk of a blood clot. One such common leg exercise may be as simple as flexing knees or ankles and rotating the feet. The patient may be given special support stockings to wear after surgery to help promote blood circulation as the nurse or doctor explain its use and purpose. Depending on the patient's medical condition, he may be given an injection to thin the blood slightly to help reduce the risk of clots.

Research shows the earlier you get out of bed and start walking, eating and drinking after the operation, the better. Hospitals would offer an enhanced recovery program if the patient had major surgery. This rehabilitation program aims to get patients back to full health quickly. It is essential to arrange for appropriate care after the operation. For older people, it is important to arrange for suitable equipment and care. Patients shouldn't be embarrassed to ask for things that may help ease up on their pain such as a wheelchair, walker, or cane.

Communication

A variety of professionals will be included in your care like physicians, nurse practitioners, physician's assistants, nurses, social workers, nursing assistants, technicians, administrative assistants and so on. You may be seen by a number of specialists here and there to help you understand in case you have questions about your care and plan for the day to be able to make decisions with the team regarding your care. Keep the information given to you in your treatment binder. Handouts about new medications, chemotherapy regimens, lab results, and test results are great additions to your treatment binder. Take notes and if something about your care does not make sense to you, ask questions until you understand. You need to be your own advocate. Having a trusted support person with you can be very helpful. This person can take notes and listen when you are being given information, taking some stress off of you and helping refresh your memory when reviewing things later.

Dress Comfortably

As long as it does not interfere with your treatment, choose to wear comfortable clothing and skid-free slippers or socks, bring a robe, a blanket and pillow from home that brings comfort to you. However, make sure that they don't get collected with the hospital laundry, otherwise they will be lost.

Hospitals are not particularly popular for their food. If you are having a difficult time with the food offered to you, ask if there is an alternative menu or special order items available. An alternative menu may include basic comfort foods, which may be more palatable. You can have family and friends bring you meals. You can keep non-perishable items like crackers, granola bars and nuts in your room. Ask the staff if/where there is a fridge available for you to keep perishable items. Frozen meals are a good option because you can heat them up in a microwave. Keep in mind the diet that your doctor prescribed you. If you have a question about the food choice within your diet, please ask your nurse or dietician.

Entertainment

Vital signs will be checked daily or health care professionals provide laboratory test. The patient's hospital stay may become monotonous that is why as caregiver, bring books, and games to help the mind to keep busy. Reading a book or newspaper can be a good distraction. Some hospitals have the option of getting the newspaper delivered each morning. You can also bring a craft or hobby to keep yourself distracted. Many hospitals provide free Wi-Fi, so bringing a laptop or other electronic devices can help pass the time. Visitors can also be entertaining, but you may also need some downtime. Skype and Face Time are other great ways to keep in touch with family and friends who cannot visit. Cell phones are welcome in most units and can save you the cost of the hospital phone.

Mental Health

Cancer and the treatment it requires can bring on many emotions, including sadness, stress, and anxiety. Being in the hospital can exacerbate these feelings, which makes it important that you take care of your mental health. Think about what makes you or the patient happy while at the hospital. Bring pictures of family, loved ones and pets to decorate the room. If you find comfort listening to music, praying, meditating or journaling, determine a time and ask your nurse to take you to where you can be uninterrupted as you do these things.

On days when you or the patient is feeling well enough, venture around the unit and see what is available. There may be support groups available on the unit, and throughout the hospital. Interacting with staff, other patients and family members will help keep you active mentally. Friendships can develop in the hospital. Other patients may be experiencing a similar diagnosis and treatment and patients can support each other in the hospital and after discharge. If you are feeling sad, speak with your medical team. Your provider or nurse can make the appropriate referrals to social work, spiritual counseling or psychiatry.

Physical Health

Treatment may require patient to be in the hospital does not mean to sit in the hospital bed all day. Patients are not recommended to be in bed all day as lying in bed the whole time is one of the worst things that you can do. On days when the care-receiver is feeling well enough, encourage him to walk in the hallways. If care recipient is not feeling up to leaving his room, caregiver can ask if there is a stationary bike available to use in the room. Advocate for the patient if the health care professionals can provide physical and occupational therapy inside the room. There may be days when you don't have the energy to get out of bed, and you may need encouragement. It is important to at least sit in a chair for a couple of hours each day to keep your muscles engaged and allow your body to move in different positions at least every three hours.

Discharge:

Before you leave the hospital, always consult with the discharge nurse and the Director of Social Services to schedule an appointment with a physiotherapist. They will be able to advise you on any exercises you need to carry out. You will also be given advice how to care for your wound, any equipment you may require, such as dressings, bandages, crutches and splints, and maybe a dose of painkillers.

Each hospital will have their own policy and arrangements for discharging patients. A discharge will be dependent on how quickly your health improves while you are in the hospital, what support needed after returning home. You won't usually be able to drive yourself home after surgery. Instead, you could ask someone to pick you up or take you home in a taxi. It's a good idea to have an adult caregiver available to help you for at least 24 hours after having a general anesthetic.

Heading Back Home

When it is time to go home, you should be given paperwork detailing your treatment course while you were in the hospital. Keep a copy in your treatment binder. Ask if you have the option to have your prescription medications filled prior to leaving or sent to a local pharmacy electronically, so they will be ready when you get there. Make sure you have contact phone numbers for any home care you have been set up with. Also, make sure your discharge paperwork notes the contact information for any providers that you need to follow up with. Appointments may have been arranged for you, all you need is to know the plan or learn the schedule.

Once home, take some time to adjust. You may have become accustomed to having staff available all hours of the day for your needs. Keeping this in mind, you may want to have a support person at home until you are used to being at home. Keep contact information available near your phone if you have any questions for your providers. You can also program the numbers directly into a cell phone. It can take some time and effort on your part to adjust to life at home, so once again, be patient.

Chapter 10

Recovery

Where To Recover After Hospitalization?

Depending on the patient's age, independence, and degree of recovery, the patient has a couple of choices, either to go back home and live independently with a caregiver for supplemental support as prescribed by the physician or to continue recovery in a skilled nursing facility on short or long term basis. Each of us may have varying degree of ability for self-care depending on age and physical attributes. Once again, a caregiver's role comes in very handy at this juncture. Going home is perhaps the best option as long as you are aware of the different community resources available to you. These resources were mentioned in the previous chapter and they are either free or with minimal cost to you. (Please see MediCal-Medicare).

Aging alone contributes to the rapid changes in the human body that may lead to unnecessary frustration and stress when a person fails to cope. Others interpret the stressors manifested by the changes as challenging behavior.

In 2019, more than 2 Million people on Medicare ended up in skilled nursing facilities after their hospitalization in California. Choosing a facility is complicated and daunting. Before discharge from the hospital, typically a nurse or a social worker hands out a list of available skilled nursing facilities in the area. The challenging part is figuring out which facility is suitable and the continuum of care provided to benefit the patient.

What is Skilled Nursing?

Upon discharge, sometimes the patient needs to recover either at home with a caregiver or if it requires extensive services, the physician may prescribe a specialized facility similar to the services provided in a hospital. Skilled Nursing Facility provides the healthcare resources you need, such as physical, occupational and speech therapy, in a supportive environment. A skilled nursing team provides around-the-clock licensed nursing care seven days per week to help you throughout your journey to recovery, whether during a long-term stay or short term rehabilitation.

Medicare covers up to 100 days of care in a skilled nursing facility (SNF) each benefit period. If you need more than 100 days of SNF care in a benefit period, you will need to pay out of pocket. If your care is ending because you are running out of days, the facility (has the option) not required to provide written notice. You or a caregiver must keep track of how many days you have spent in the SNF to avoid unexpected costs after Medicare coverage ends. Remember that you can again become eligible for Medicare coverage of your SNF care, once you have been out of a hospital or SNF for (60) sixty straight days in a row. You will then be eligible for a new benefit period, including 100 new days of SNF care, after a three-day qualifying inpatient stay.

If you are receiving medically necessary physical, occupational, or speech therapy, Medicare may continue to cover those skilled therapy services even when you have used up your SNF days in a benefit period but Medicare will not pay for your room and board, meaning you may face high costs. Check with your Insurance provider if you qualify for therapy at home through Medicare's home health benefit, or if you could safely receive therapy as an outpatient while living at home either the services come to you or you visit the clinics.

If you have long-term care insurance, it may cover your SNF stay after your Medicare coverage ends. Check with your plan for more information. If your income is low, you may be eligible for Medicaid to cover your care. To find out if you meet eligibility requirements in your state, contact your local Medicaid office.

The Two Types of Skilled Nursing Care:
Short-Term Care and Long Term Care

Short-term care programs are designed to provide you with temporary care after life events such as surgery, illness or accident. With round-the-clock, licensed nursing care and a variety of physical, speech and occupational therapies, the team of health care professionals can help you get back to your normal life as soon as possible. The program may include the following:

- Cardiac care
- Orthopedic care
- Stroke recovery care
- Pulmonary care
- Wound care
- Diabetes care
- Transplant care
- Nutrition therapy
- Pain management
- Intravenous therapy

Long-Term Care

In addition to short-term recovery and rehabilitation programs, the skilled nursing facility may also provide long-term care if you or a your loved one needs 24-hour nursing care on an on-going basis and access to a range of physical, speech and occupational therapies. Some other communities offer respite, palliative, home health, and hospice care in a warm and supportive environment designed to keep you or your loved one as comfortable as possible.

Skilled Nursing Services

Each patient in a skilled nursing facility has unique needs and circumstances. Facilities shall provide a comprehensive range of advanced medical resources to make sure everyone receives the quality care they deserve. From round-the-clock care and on-site rehabilitation professionals to assistance with daily activities, trained teams are available seven days a week to support you in your recovery. And because life doesn't come to a halt just because you're in skilled nursing, you can even take advantage of amenities like daily events calendar, quality dining program and entertainment programs.

Here are a few of the services that are often available in a skilled nursing facility:

- Skilled Nursing
- Post-surgical Care
- Medication Management
- Pain Management
- Wound Care
- Oxygen Therapy
- Continence Care
- Catheter Care
- Colostomy Care
- Nutrition and Hydration Programs
- Diabetes Care
- Cardiac Care
- CVA/Stroke Care
- Infectious Diseases
- Joint Replacement/Fracture Care
- IV Therapy/TPN/Antibiotic Management
- Rehabilitation
- Physical Therapy
- Occupational Therapy
- Speech Therapy
- Orthopedic Rehab
- Neurologic Rehab for Stroke, Multiple Sclerosis, and Parkinson's
- Fall Prevention Program
- Dysphagia/Swallowing Program (VitalStim)
- Adaptive/Assistive Equipment
- Activities of Daily Living Re-training

- Home Assessment/Visit for a Safe Discharge
- Balance and Vestibular Therapy

What are the different programs available when I am discharged from the hospital?

There are several programs available in the community that you can avail upon discharge. The samples presented here are mere estimates to give you a general idea of the programs and their respective cost in California which is comparable or cheaper depending on the state where you live. This information will come in handy, particularly when the recipient of care is an adult or an elderly.

California Assisted Living: The average cost of assisted living in California in 2019 is $4,500/month. However, based on the geographic region of the state, the average monthly cost ranges from $3,150 to $5,595. In the most expensive areas of the state; Marin County, which includes the San Francisco area, San Jose, San Luis Obispo, Santa Cruz, and Napa, the monthly estimated cost ranges from $5,425 - $5,595. The least expensive assisted living can be found inland cities and counties, in the cities of Bakersfield, Madera, Merced, Stockton, and Modesto. In these areas, the average monthly cost is between $3,150 and $3,500. Alzheimer's residential care, also called Memory Care, can add as much as $900 to $1,350 to the monthly cost of assisted living.

California Home Care: In 2019, the average hourly rate for home care across California is $26.00 per hour. As with the cost of assisted living, the average range across the state is large. On the low end, in-home care can be found at $22.50/hour, and on the high end, in-home care can be as much as $31.00 / hour. The least expensive city for home care are Chico, Visalia, Vallejo, and Riverside, where the average cost is closer to $22.50- $24.00/ hour. In Napa, San Jose, Santa Rosa, and El Centro, the cost is approximately $29.50 - $31.00/hour.

California Adult Day Care: Adult day care is the most affordable care option for seniors. In 2019, the average daily cost is $78. In Chico, San Jose, and Santa

Rosa, it is more expensive, ranging from $92 - $109 / day. The least expensive areas of the state for adult day care are Hanford, Vallejo, and Visalia. Here, the average cost of adult day care is $40 - $63/day. Several areas have costs slightly below the state's average daily cost and include the following: Los Angeles, Modesto, Merced, Salinas, Riverside, and Fresno. In these areas, the average daily cost for adult day care is between $70 and $77/day.

California Financial Assistance Programs: Medi-Cal Programs for the Elderly: Medicaid in California is called Medi-Cal. It is a program for disabled and elderly individuals and persons with limited income and resources. Through Medi-Cal, some personal care and nursing home care is provided. As part of Medi-Cal, there is an In-Home Supportive Services (IHSS) Program. The state Medicaid program, non-medical care is provided for eligible elderly individuals to prevent or delay nursing home placement. Services and benefits may include assistance with daily living activities, housecleaning, meal preparation, and grocery shopping, to name a few. The program is an entitlement, meaning if one meets the eligibility requirements, the services may be provided. This program allows individuals to choose the provider and services of their choice, including family members and even spouses.

Medicaid "waivers": Also referred to as Home and Community Based Services (HCBS) waivers, are available that provide assistance for home care, adult day care, home modifications, and assisted living. These programs are also in place to help prevent nursing home placements. Unlike the state Medicaid plan, Medicaid waivers are not entitlement programs. This means there are enrollment caps for program participation, and if the cap has been reached, a waitlist for services will exist.

Assisted Living Waiver Program (ALWP): helps individuals who are eligible for nursing home care, but would prefer to live in an assisted living community. While room and board are not covered, several supportive services are available, such as personal care assistance, medication administration, and prepared meals.

Multipurpose Senior Services Program (MSSP) Waiver helps nursing home eligible individuals that prefer to stay in their homes continue to do so. It covers care management and supportive services, such as adult day care, assistive technology, and home modifications, but doesn't pay for medical care. This program, unfortunately, is not available in every county of California.

The Home and Community-Based Alternatives (HCBA) Waiver, previously called the Medi-Cal Nursing Facility / Acute Hospital (NF/AH) Waiver, is a combination of several former waivers that helps nursing home eligible individuals receive care services, including medical care in their homes. This program also offers assistance to individuals currently residing in nursing facilities who wish to move back to their home.

Medi-Cal's Adult Day Health Care program has transitioned into the newly created Community Based Adult Services (CBAS) program. This program provides daytime care, meals, social activities, therapies, and skilled nursing. Functional needs must be met.

In order to qualify for the state Medicaid plan or one of the waivers, Medi-Cal has both income and asset qualifications. These limits depend on one's age and marital status. As of 2019, a single elderly individual's monthly income cannot exceed approximately $1,242, or $1,682 as a married couple. An individual can qualify for Medi-Cal if the total value of their assets does not exceed $2,000, and for a married couple, $3,000. One's home (CA is unique in that there is no equity value limit), household furnishings, burial plots, personal effects, and a vehicle are not included in the asset calculation.

Persons with income and assets over these limits can still become eligible for Medi-Cal assistance. Individuals whose income exceeds the limit(s), but who have high medical expenses may qualify through a Medi-Cal spend-down program called Share of Cost. Persons with assets valued over the limit might become eligible by working with a Medi-Cal planner to structure their resources appropriately. If there is some question regarding qualification, it is strongly recommended individuals contact a Medi-Cal Planner prior to application. This especially holds true if one is over the income and / or asset limit(s).

State (Non-Medicaid) Assistance Programs: California also offers assistance programs for the elderly that do not require an individual to qualify for Medicaid (Medi-Cal). Unfortunately, in 2012, the state's budget for Alzheimer's Day Care Resource Centers (ADCRC) was cut. However, some Area Agency on Aging offices may have funding to assist with adult daycare costs.

California Paid Family Leave. This program provides up to six weeks paid time off for working professionals, specifically to care for a family member. Finally, for San Francisco residents, a local, pilot program called Support at Home provides financial assistance for elderly individuals or disabled persons to help them remain living in their homes.

Financial Options for Care: In addition to these state specific options that help pay for care, there are many non-profit and federal options. Use our Resource Locator Tool to find other programs that help pay for or reduce the cost of care. There are also programs that help veterans with assisted living, and there are eldercare loans available in California. While reverse mortgages are available nationwide, California's real estate values have resulted in a unique financial product. This is an alternative to a reverse mortgage and can be used to pay for elder care for some families. These are just a few known resources that are available in the community but may not be seen in other counties and states. The program costs stated may vary and changes depending on the state and federal budget available from time to time.

Nutrition

In the age we live, there is an unprecedented focus on getting and staying healthy. As more and more research points to the effect of fitness and nutrition on our overall health, the findings become more difficult to ignore. There is no doubt that the food we eat and the physical activity that we perform significantly impact our weight and our body's overall health and longevity.

Nutrition is defined as the intake of food, considered in relation to the body's dietary needs.

- Good nutrition: an adequate, well balanced diet combined with regular physical activity is a cornerstone of good health.

- Poor nutrition can lead to reduced immunity, increased susceptibility to disease, impaired physical and mental development, and reduced productivity.

A healthy diet includes the preparation of food and storage methods that preserve nutrients from oxidation, heat or leaching, and that reduce risk of food-born illnesses. Diet and nutrition refers to the intake of food and nourishment for the growth and maintenance of the body. Dietitians or nutritionists consider a diet as a balanced meal that contains appropriate portions of all nutrients. A good diet helps a person to maintain good health. Fitness is the overall well being of the human body. Diet and nutrition are therefore an important part of fitness.

The escalating rate of workplace disabilities is causing businesses and consumers alike to revisit how they handle stress and health issues. High stress, lack of exercise and other factors exacerbated by an aging U.S. workforce are contributing to an increase in the numbers of individuals receiving long-term disability payments each year, according to a new study from the Council for Disability Awareness.

Fitness and Nutrition Equal Good Health

When we keep our bodies active through a consistent exercise program, we are adding to our body's ability to metabolize food and keep weight down. Further, good fitness means strong and limber muscles and a strong cardiovascular system. Exercise also lowers blood pressure and reduces stress levels.

When you look at fitness and nutrition and the consequences of ignoring their importance, it is not difficult to see how large a role they play in our health.

It is important to understand how powerfully diet can affect us. Natural, whole foods, such as fresh vegetables, fruits, whole grains, and lean proteins give our bodies the vitamins and minerals we need to function effectively. We have energy when we eat right and burn fat. Eating properly allows us to maintain a healthy weight and keep undue stress off our hearts; it also allows us to keep our blood pressure and cholesterol levels healthy. Most importantly, good nutrition keeps our bodies stocked with antioxidants that fight off a range of illnesses including cancer.

Regular exercise is one of the requirements necessary to address health and fitness issues. The types of exercises that will improve and strengthen the heart muscles are highly recommended.

If you spend long hours in a wheelchair you know it can lead to uneasiness and can be very uncomfortable. Keeping the body moving as much as possible in your wheelchair should be a regular part of your daily fitness program. This should be a priority no matter what your disability. Doing regular wheelchair exercise will help you increase your strength, flexibility, improve your mobility, strengthen your heart and lungs, and control your weight.

Keep Body Moving

- Burn your excess fat and calories.
- Mental stimulation and exercise can be incorporated to keep you mind sharp and sound.
- Challenge your mind to grow, expand, learn, explore, decipher, and experience.
- Meditation can reduce stress, heart rate, and blood pressure.

Researchers studied 370 members of a runners club aged 50 years and older, and 249 community members who did not belong to the running club. They were between 50 and 72 years of age at the start of the 13-year study. The runners had far lower death rates, which was expected, and far less disability, such as osteoarthritis, which is impressive.

Basic Nutrition Facts

- Adding Sugar is a Disaster.
- Unprocessed Food is Healthiest.
- There is no Perfect Diet For Everyone.
- Refined Carbohydrates are Bad For You.
- Eating Vegetables Will Improve Your Health.
- It is Critical to Avoid Vitamin D Deficiency.
- Supplements Can Never Fully Replace Real Foods

- "Diets" Don't Work, a Lifestyle Change is Necessary.
- Omega-3 Fats Are Crucial and Most People Don't Get Enough.
- Artificial Trans Fats Are Very Unhealthy and Should be Avoided.

Assisted Independence

Assistive Technology. There are literally thousands of assistive devices available out there to make your life manageable in maintaining independence at home and in the community despite physical limitations.

(1). **Medication Reminder Pill Bottles:** These bottles have a recorder that vocalize instructions on how to take medications and what to do when you miss a dose. The pharmacist actually records the message. Average Price: $25.00.

(2). **Vibrating Watch:** Vibrating watches are wonderful to remind one's scheduled meeting, when to take medication or and other activities. Average Price: $100.00.

(3). **Talking Cooking Thermometer** (not just for cooking): There are many uses for this item such as for in the kitchen testing the temperature of the meat or when cooking water. Other uses include testing the temperature of a room, bathwater, and heating pads. Average Price: $30.00.

(4). **Braille Speaker-phone with Large Numbers:** Phones of these types have large numbers with accompanying symbols in Braille as well as a visual ring indicator. Average Price: $33.00.

(5). **Checks and Deposit Register:** Checks in Large Print can be ordered for free from your local bank. Large check registers measuring 8.5 by 11 for the visually impaired are available for purchase. They make it easy to maintain your finances. Average Price $6.00.

(6). **Talking Timers:** There are many types that mention the end of timing. Some come with many different functions but of course the cost is much more. The price below is for the basic ones. The Average Price: $12.00.

(7). **Talking Color Identifier:** This is an invaluable wonder tool for identifying colors that is preformed by placing the tool on the item. The color is then identified in speech. Items that the tool can be used on are clothing, fabric or many other surfaces. There are 14 types of colors normally identified with these products. Average Price: $140.00.

(8). **Talking Calculators:** They have large print and also speak. The lower priced ones have the basic functions of adding, subtracting, dividing, multiplying, and calculating percentages. Average Price: $20.00.

(9). **Talking Books and Players**: These are available for free through the Talking Books Services. Check your local Agencies.

(10). **White Canes:** Most canes come in carbon fiber for lasting quality. They are best as collapsing types for they fit conveniently anywhere. Average Price: $35.00

(11). **Talking Clocks and Watches:** There are several types of talking clocks and watches with excellent voice quality. Average Price: $15.00.

(12). **Magnifiers**: Magnifiers come is several sizes with different magnification depending upon what the user's needs. Prices do vary. Average Price: $10.00

(13). **Braille Tags:** These are great for sewing into clothes to identify them. An example would be to determine the color or for matching purposes. They come in a package. Typically the amount is a quantity of 50. Average Price: $30.00

(14). **Low Browse:** From Lighthouse International this is an add-on to Mozilla's Firefox browser. It enables a visually impaired person to view web pages as the web author intended them to be viewed. This software also reads the text on those pages that is formatted to the viewer's own needs.

20/20 Vision

A term used to express normal visual acuity (the clarity or sharpness of vision) measured at a distance of 20 feet. If you have 20/20 vision, you can see clearly at 20 feet what should normally be seen at that distance. If you have 20/40 vision, it means that when you stand 20 feet away from the chart you can see what a normal human eye can see when standing 40 feet from the chart.

Legally Blind:

In North America and most of Europe, legal blindness is defined as visual acuity (vision) of 20/200 (6/60) or less in the better eye with best correction possible. A a legally blind individual would have to stand 20 feet (6 m) from an object to see it with the same degree of clarity as a normally sighted person could from 200 feet (60 m).

Statistics: Vision Impairment

- 80% of all visual impairment can be prevented or cured.
- 82% of people living with blindness are aged 50 and above.
- About 90% of the world's visually impaired live in low-income settings.
- 285 million people are estimated to be visually impaired worldwide: 39 million are blind and 246 have low vision.

According to global estimates, the number of people visually impaired from infectious diseases has reduced in the last 20 years. Globally, uncorrected refractive errors are the leading cause of moderate to severe visual impairment; cataracts remain the leading cause of blindness in middle and low-income countries.

What is Assistive Technology?

Assistive technology (AT) is a general term that includes assistive, adaptive, and rehabilitative devices for people with disabilities. In this section, there is a provision including the process used in selecting, locating, and using them. Assistive technology promotes greater independence by enabling people to perform tasks that they were formerly unable to accomplish, or had great difficulty accomplishing, by providing enhancements to, or changing methods of interacting with, the technology needed to accomplish such tasks. Assistive technology products are designed to provide additional accessibility to individuals who have physical or cognitive difficulties, impairments, and disabilities. There are so many instances where, minor modifications alone can make a mainstream product accessible to anyone. Nevertheless, there are also situations where your only option is assistive technology. Most of the time, Medical and Medicare or private insurance pays for these devises.

Is Adaptive Technology the Same as Assistive technology?

The term adaptive technology is often used as the synonym for assistive technology; however, they are different terms. Assistive technology refers to "any item, piece of equipment, or product system, whether acquired commercially, modified, or customized, that is used to increase, maintain, or improve functional capabilities of individuals with disabilities", while adaptive technology covers items that are specifically designed for persons with disabilities and would seldom be used by non-disabled persons.

If you have a disability or injury, you may use a number of assistive devices or rehabilitation equipment to aid you in and around the home. Assistive devices are tools, products or types of equipment that help you perform tasks and activities if you have a disability, injury or are a senior. Assistive devices may help you move around, see, communicate, eat, or get dressed/undressed.

Assistive devices for mobility/ambulation can also be referred to as ambulatory aids. Ambulatory aids (eg, canes, crutches, walkers) are used to provide an extension of the upper extremities to help transmit body weight and provide support for the user. Assistive devices can help you improve your quality of life and maintain your sense of independence.

Well designed high quality assistive devices, or daily living aids, that support independent living for the handicapped and disabled, seniors, or those with a medical condition or injury should make life easier and safer for the aged and disabled.

AT promotes greater independence by enabling people to perform tasks that they were formerly unable to accomplish, or had great difficulty accomplishing, by providing enhancements to or changed methods of interacting with the technology needed to accomplish such tasks.

An assistive device could be a wheelchair, translator, voice over interphase, Artificial Intelligence or an equipment/product that allows you to use a computer. If you experience difficulties performing specific tasks, it is possible that an assistive device can help you overcome your problems.

Other Disability Aids Include

- Advanced walking technology products to aid people with disabilities, such as paraplegia or cerebral palsy, who would not at all able to walk or stand (exoskeletons).
- Standing products to support people with disabilities in the standing position while maintaining/improving their health (standing frame, standing wheelchair, active stander).
- Seating products that assist people to sit comfortably and safely (seating systems, cushions, therapeutic seats).
- Walking products to aid people with disabilities who are able to walk or stand with assistance (canes, crutches, walkers, gait trainers).
- Wheeled mobility products that enable people with reduced mobility to move freely indoors and outdoors (Examples: wheelchairs and scooters).

Certain devices, such as eyeglasses and hearing aids, obviously require an expert's assessment, but many assistive devices for the enhancement of daily life such as wheelchairs, walkers, bath seats and grab bars, eating utensils are easily obtainable in general and specialty stores including online disability product websites.

Pharmacy personnel are usually quite happy to provide information on a variety of other assistive products like magnifying glasses, bath seats, joint support bandages, pill organizers, canes, etc.

Specialty computer stores often carry items like screen reading software that include screen enlargement features for persons with vision impairments. Voice recognition systems, modified keyboards and computer mice are also available for people with mobility and dexterity limitations.

When selecting assistive technology products for computers, it is crucial to find the right products that are compatible with the computer operating system and programs on the particular computer you will be using.

What Does the Future Hold for Assistive Technology?

This is a very exciting time for new developments in assistive technology. Not only are existing AT programs regularly updated, but new and previously unseen technology is on-route to improve accessibility for persons with disabilities. With the advent of e-book readers like the Kindle, Sony E-reader, and recently the Nook released by Barnes and Noble, there could be another wave of new methods for people with learning disabilities and other conditions to access e-books and books. While not all of the devices have text-to-speech capability, some of them do, and if it proves useful, other producers of e-book readers will probably follow suit and adopt that utility in the near future.

By current estimates, more than 4,000 assistive technologies have been designed for the disabled and seniors. These devices include everything from wheelchairs to a wide assortment of high-tech tools and many companies today are turning their research and development to assistive technologies.

Home Automation

The form of home automation called assistive domotics focuses on making it possible for elderly and disabled people to live independently. Home automation is becoming a viable option for the elderly and disabled who would prefer to stay in their own homes rather than move to a healthcare facility. This field uses much of the same technology and equipment as home automation for security, entertainment, and energy conservation but tailors it towards elderly and disabled users.

If you think you could benefit from using an assistive device, start by consulting a healthcare professional, such as your doctor, pharmacist, or an occupational therapist. Find out what is available to suit your needs. You can also obtain information about assistive devices from catalogs and seniors' magazines. Don't let your disability or sensory loss infringe on your lifestyle, especially when tools and devices exist to help you overcome these obstacles.

Chapter 11

Guardianship v. Conservatorship

A s we go on to a more sensitive subject close to aging, disability and death, nobody wants to talk about the issue of who is going to take care of us and our personal belongings, who will decide when we are partially or totally incapacitated or most specially who is going to make life changing decisions when we are not able to especially if close to dying or when we die? Such dreadful subjects are too personal to deal with but we need to accept them as they are when that day comes. For me, the subject must be discussed as soon as possible whether there is some form of assets involved or not, any family member or significant other may be impacted by our uncertain future.

Generally, guardianship and conservatorship are interchangeable and similar in purpose and objective but technically different in meaning and application depending in the state where you live. In California, guardianship is used a lot in children from infants up to the age of eighteen. When they become adults and they are developmentally and mentally incapacitated and unable to make self-determination, a public/state agency such as Adult Protective Services, Department of Aging or a state-federal agency such as Regional Center has to step in to protect their personal and financial interest especially when they have assets to support their medical needs under conservatorship.

Guardian

A guardian of the person is responsible for decisions about care provisions and living arrangements of the ward. A guardian of the estate, also known as a conservator, is charged with the ward's property and financial affairs.

Everyone wants to live an independent life in which they are able manage their own affairs. However, as we all age or become disabled mentally or physically we may one day live a life when we become dependent on others to assist us from simple task to making major decisions in life. In such cases, we might need to consider preparing ourselves for the inevitable. Conservatorship and guardianship are legal tools that we can use to help us protect ourselves or a child's well-being. Both processes involve court proceedings in which a judge appoints conservator or guardian the responsibility for making various decisions on an incapacitated person's behalf. Such decisions may be of a legal, medical, financial or personal nature.

In California, guardianship refers only to the court appointment of an individual with the legal authority to represent and manage the affairs of a minor child. This can be achieved by applying a petition in Family Court or Superior Court in the county where you live. Conservatorships are for protecting incapacitated adults and typically involve matters related to health care and estate. Many states use the term "guardianship" instead of "conservatorship" when referring to the same duties for adults. In these states "conservator" refers to someone appointed only to handle finances. California courts typically establish guardianships if both parents are unable to provide a child with a safe and secure home due to death, mental disability or other circumstances. Such arrangements allow a guardian to make decisions for the child until they are of legal age to care for themselves.

The need for a conservatorship may arise when an adult individual experiences an injury, accident or other health event that causes them to become incapacitated. They may also require assistance in various areas of life after becoming mentally incapacitated due to disability or old age.

The process of issuing a conservatorship or guardianship is often difficult, costly and time-consuming. Conservatorship should be viewed as a last resort when a Durable Power of Attorney or Advance Health Care Directive has not been signed. Otherwise, it can impose significant limitations on a person's ability to maintain their independence and freedom.

There are many differences between a Conservatorship and a Power of Attorney. One difference is that a POA is typically set up prior to an individual becoming incapacitated, while a Conservatorship typically comes into effect after an individual becomes incapacitated.

Revocable Living Trust and Power of Attorney Power of Attorney

Making financial and legal decisions for aging loved ones can be overwhelming for any caregiver. Knowing where to start and how to make those decisions can be complex and can come with heavy emotional stress. Having a power of attorney is one of the first steps to making important decisions with your loved one easier. Recognized by the court, a power of attorney can eliminate some caregiver stress as loved ones age and become unable to make their own legal and financial decisions.

A power of attorney does not remove your power to act, it just authorizes someone else to also act under the limitations that you have placed. It is not the same as a conservatorship, where a court removes your power to act and places that power in the hands of another.

What is a Power of Attorney?

Simply put, a power of attorney (POA) is a legal document that gives another person or organization the legal right to handle the affairs of someone no longer available or unable to do so. There are four different kinds of powers of attorney:

General Power of Attorney

A general power of attorney enables someone to act on the behalf of someone else in a variety of situations including handling of one's affairs.

Special Power of Attorney

A special power of attorney outlines specific circumstances where one is authorized to act on the behalf of someone else (i.e. selling a car, selling a home, borrowing money).

Power of Attorney for Health Care

A health care power of attorney allows someone else to make health care decisions if the person affected is no longer able to do so. This is found in the sample at the end of this chapter.

Durable Power of Attorney

General, special, and health care powers of attorney can be made "durable", meaning that the document will remain in effect or take effect if the person becomes mentally incompetent to make his or her own decisions. It is not recommended that seniors use an ordinary or non-durable POA. These types of POA's automatically end if your loved one should become incapacitated – which is when families need their POA most.

How and When To Obtain Power of Attorney

It is best for caregivers to obtain a POA as soon as they notice their loved one's health is failing. Because all parties must fully comprehend the document's effects, it is best to get the document executed before progressive diseases like dementia worsen. Many families wait until it is too late to get a POA. If the senior does not have any durable POAs and they have a health emergency, the family may end up in court to battle for the authority to handle their loved ones financial and health decisions. In an actual emergency with no POA, a stranger may end up making these important decisions for your loved one. It is important to note that a power of attorney does not give another individual complete sovereignty over another individual's finances, assets, or healthcare. Each power of attorney can be modified so that clear language lays out exactly what the power of attorney is allowing another individual to control.

To obtain a power of attorney, the person granting power of attorney must be mentally competent and able to understand exactly what rights they are giving to someone else over their estate, health, and affairs. For durable powers of attorney, certain requirements can be detailed that would bring the POA into effect.

Most attorneys can create a POA and notarize the document, which will help ensure the validity of the document over time. Some states offer online forms that would give powers of attorney to another individual, but requirements for obtaining a POA differ in each state so it is best to contact a legal professional who is licensed in your state to ensure the document is executed correctly.

Revocable Living Trust

Life is uncertain that we do not know what lies ahead as we can get sick, be involved in an accident, or even die anytime today or tomorrow. It is always wise to plan ahead and figure out who will take care of us, who will make health care decisions, and who will take care of our property in case something serious happens. One best way is to prepare a Revocable Living Trust. A revocable living trust is a popular estate planning tool that you can use to determine who will get your property when you die.

Most living trusts are "revocable" because you can change them as your circumstances or wishes change. Revocable living trusts are "living" because you make them during your lifetime. Lawyers sometimes call this "inter vivos." Even if a Trust can be personally created, it is better to consult an attorney or a paralegal as there are some complex verbiage and instructions that a trust needs to indicate in order to avoid possibility of complication and claim for probate. Attorneys can walk you through each step in the process from preparing a trust and beyond. However, there are sample trusts that can be found online and even comes with instructions how to prepare it. In this chapter, I have included a sample Revocable Trust that you can read to have an idea on how you can prepare your own trust.

Revocable Living Trusts to Avoid Probate.

Most people use living trusts to avoid probate. Probate is the court-supervised process of wrapping up a person's estate. Probate can be expensive, time consuming, and is often more of a burden than a help. Property left through a living trust can pass to beneficiaries without probate. A living trust document is a legal written document that is signed by the maker of the trust and a notary public. The document must list the property in the trust, name a trustee, and name an individual who gets the property when the maker of trust dies. The trustee is the person who will take care of the property. While the trust maker is alive, the trustee is usually the trust maker and then a successor trustee takes over after the trust maker's death.

Transferring Property Into the Trust.

After the trust document is made, the trust maker must transfer any property he or she wants covered by the trust into the trust. For many items, this requires simply including a list of property with the trust document. However, titled property (like real estate) must be retitled in the name of the trust. This is usually not complicated or difficult, but it must be done correctly or the titled property could end up in probate. There are also computer softwares that you can pay and download into your computer so you can create a living trust quickly and easily such as Nolo's Quicken WillMaker Plus software.

Revocable Living Trusts v. Wills

With both wills and revocable living trusts you can: (a) name beneficiaries for property; (b). leave property to young children; and (c). revise your document as your circumstances or wishes change.

With a trust, not a will, you can: (*) Avoid probate; (*) reduce the chance of a court dispute over your estate; (*) avoid a conservatorship; and keep your document private after death.

With a will, not a trust, you can: (*) name guardians for children; (*) name managers for children's property; (*) name an executor; and (*) instruct how debts or taxes should be paid.

Do You Need A Lawyer to Make a Trust?

You do not have to be a lawyer to make a living trust. If you have a fairly straightforward situation and you are willing to do the work, you can make your own revocable living trust. However, some situations warrant seeing a lawyer for help, so always consult with a lawyer. However, if you can not afford one, here is a sample of a trust that was prepared for me by my lawyer and feel free to modify it according to your need.

In the succeeding pages, you will find a sample Revocable Living Trust made by my lawyer for my family which I deleted my personal information and left blank for you to use as a guide in writing your own trust. However, I advise you to see an advocate, paralegal or an estate attorney who can properly assist you with your estate planning as laws vary in every state.

Conclusion

Beyond caregiving is about sympathy and genuine understanding of a person's needs when one is in a state when no one is there for them. It is about endurance and patience to be able to face life's challenges, a test of faith in self and in human kindness of others. When the challenge is beyond our realm, we have to trust in GOD and his plan for each and every one of us. Although we are now aware of other alternatives in care and community available resources at our disposal, it is still purely up to us to make a difference to ourselves and to the community we live in. Positivity, knowledge and optimism are the key elements that could unlock our freedom to live happy normal lives that God has intended for us to enjoy. Tell family, friends and others that you love them before it is too late. I hope that this book has shared important information to you, so, now it is your time to share it to others.

Sample Guide on How to Prepare A Revocable Living Trust

Declaration of Trust

Part 1. Trust Name

This revocable living trust shall be known as the ___John MakerTrust Revocable Living Trust____.

Part 2. Declaration of Trust

John MakerTrust, called the grantor, declares that she has transferred and delivered to the trustee all her interest in the property described in Schedule A attached to this Declaration of Trust. All of that property is

157

called the "trust property." The trustee hereby acknowledges receipt of the trust property and agrees to hold the trust property in trust, according to this Declaration of Trust.

The grantor may add property to the trust.

Part 3. Terminology

The term "this Declaration of Trust" includes any provisions added by valid amendment.

Part 4. Amendment and Revocation

A. Amendment or Revocation by Grantor

The grantor may amend or revoke this trust at any time, without notifying any beneficiary. An amendment must be made in writing and signed by the grantor. Revocation may be in writing or any manner allowed by law.

B. Amendment or Revocation by Other Person

The power to revoke or amend this trust is personal to the grantor. A conservator, guardian or other person shall not exercise it on behalf of the grantor, unless the grantor specifically grants a power to revoke or amend this trust in a Durable Power of Attorney.

Part 5. Payments From Trust During Grantor's Lifetime

The trustee shall pay to or use for the benefit of the grantor as much of the net income and principal of the trust property as the grantor requests. Income shall be paid to the grantor at least annually. Income accruing in or paid to trust accounts shall be deemed to have been paid to the grantor.

Part 6. Trustees

A. Trustee

John MakerTrust shall be the trustee of this trust.

B. Trustee's Responsibilities

The trustee in office shall serve as trustee of all trusts created under this Declaration of Trust, including children's subtrusts.

C. Terminology

In this Declaration of Trust, the term "trustee" includes successor trustees or alternate successor trustees serving as trustee of this trust. The singular "trustee" also includes the plural.

D. Successor Trustee

Upon the death or incapacity of John MakerTrust, the trustee of this trust and of any children's subtrusts created by it shall be Peter Favorite. If Peter Favorite is unable or unwilling to serve as successor trustee, Mary Second shall serve as trustee.

E. Resignation of Trustee

Any trustee in office may resign at any time by signing a notice of resignation. The resignation shall be delivered to the person or institution who is either named in this Declaration of Trust, or appointed by the trustee under Section F of this Part, to next serve as the trustee.

F. Power to Appoint Successor Trustee

If no one named in this Declaration of Trust as a successor trustee or alternate successor trustee is willing or able to serve as trustee, the last acting trustee may appoint a successor trustee and may require the posting of a reasonable bond, to be paid for from the trust property. The appointment must be made in writing, signed by the trustee and notarized.

G. Bond

No bond shall be required for any trustee named in this Declaration of Trust.

H. Compensation

No trustee shall receive any compensation for serving as trustee, unless the trustee serves as a trustee of a child's subtrust created by this Declaration of Trust.

I. Liability of Trustee

With respect to the exercise or non-exercise of discretionary powers granted by this Declaration of Trust, the trustee shall not be liable for actions taken in good faith. Such actions shall be binding on all persons interested in the trust property.

Part 7. Trustee's Management Powers and Duties

A. Powers Under State Law

The trustee shall have all authority and powers allowed or conferred on a trustee under (State) law, subject to the trustee's fiduciary duty to the grantors and the beneficiaries.

B. Specified Powers

The trustee's powers include, but are not limited to:

- The power to sell trust property, and to borrow money and to encumber trust property, including trust real estate, by mortgage, deed of trust or other method.
- The power to manage trust real estate as if the trustee were the absolute owner of it, including the power to lease (even if the lease term may extend beyond the period of any trust) or grant options to lease the property, to make repairs or alterations and to insure against loss.
- The power to sell or grant options for the sale or exchange of any trust property, including stocks, bonds, debentures and

any other form of security or security account, at public or private sale for cash or on credit.

- The power to invest trust property in every kind of property and every kind of investment, including but not limited to bonds, debentures, notes, mortgages, stock options, futures and stocks, and including buying on margin.
- The power to receive additional property from any source and add it to any trust created by this Declaration of Trust.
- The power to employ and pay reasonable fees to accountants, lawyers or investment experts for information or advice relating to the trust.
- The power to deposit and hold trust funds in both interest-bearing and non-interest-bearing accounts.
- The power to deposit funds in bank or other accounts uninsured by FDIC coverage.
- The power to enter into electronic fund transfer or safe deposit arrangements with financial institutions.
- The power to continue any business of the grantor.
- The power to institute or defend legal actions concerning this trust or the grantor's affairs.
- The power to execute any documents necessary to administer any trust created by this Declaration of Trust.
- The power to diversify investments, including authority to decide that some or all of the trust property need not produce income.

Part 8. Incapacity of Grantor

If the grantor becomes physically or mentally incapacitated, whether or not a court has declared the grantor incompetent or in need of a conservator or guardian, the successor trustee named in Part 6 shall be trustee.

The determination of the grantor's capacity to manage this trust shall be made by Betty Thirdly. The successor trustee shall, if necessary, ask Betty Thirdly to state, in writing, an opinion as to whether or not the grantor is able to continue serving as trustee. The successor trustee may rely on that written opinion when determining whether or not to begin serving as trustee.

If the successor trustee is unable, after making reasonable efforts, to obtain a written opinion from Betty Thirdly, the successor trustee may request an opinion from Armand Fourth and may rely on that opinion.

If the successor trustee is also unable, after making reasonable efforts, to obtain a written opinion from _____, the successor trustee may request an opinion from _____ and may rely on that opinion.

If the successor trustee is unable, after making reasonable efforts, to obtain a written opinion from _____, _____, or _____, the successor trustee may request an opinion from a physician who examines the grantor, and may rely on that opinion.

The trustee shall use any amount of trust income or trust property necessary for the grantor's proper health care, support, maintenance, comfort and welfare, in accordance with the grantor's accustomed manner of living. Any income not spent for the benefit of the grantor shall be accumulated and added to the trust property. Income shall be paid to the grantor at least annually. Income accruing in or paid to trust accounts shall be deemed to have been paid to the grantor.

The successor trustee shall manage the trust until the grantor is again able to manage her affairs. The determination of the grantor's capacity to again manage this trust shall be made in the manner specified just above.

Part 9. Death of a Grantor

When the grantor dies, this trust shall become irrevocable. It may not be amended or altered except as provided for by this Declaration of Trust. It may be terminated only by the distributions authorized by this Declaration of Trust.

The trustee may pay out of trust property such amounts as necessary for payment of the grantor's debts, estate taxes and expenses of the grantor's last illness and funeral.

Part 10. Beneficiaries

At the death of the grantor, the trustee shall distribute the trust property as follows:

_____ shall be given John MakerTrust interest in 100 shares of_____ stock. If_____ does not survive John MakerTrust, that property shall be given to _____.

_____ shall be given John MakerTrust interest in the trust property not otherwise specifically and validly disposed of by this Part. If _____ does not survive John MakerTrust, that property shall be given to _____.

Part 11. Terms of Property Distribution

All distributions are subject to any provision in this Declaration of Trust that creates a child's subtrust or a custodianship under the Uniform Transfers to Minors Act.

A beneficiary must survive the grantor for 120 hours to receive property under this Declaration of Trust. As used in this Declaration of Trust, to survive means to be alive or in existence as an organization.

All personal and real property left through this trust shall pass subject to any encumbrances or liens placed on the property as security for the repayment of a loan or debt.

If property is left to two or more beneficiaries to share, they shall share it equally unless this Declaration of Trust provides otherwise. If any of them does not survive the grantor, the others shall take that beneficiary's share, to share equally, unless this Declaration of Trust provides otherwise.

Part 12. Custodianships Under the Uniform Transfers to Minors Act

Any property to which _____ becomes entitled under Part 10 of this Declaration of Trust shall be given to _____ as custodian for _____ under the California Uniform Transfers to Minors Act, until _____ reaches the age of 21. If _____ is unable or ceases to serve as custodian, _____ shall serve as custodian.

Part 13. Grantor's Right to Homestead Tax Exemption

If the grantor's principal residence is held in trust, the grantor has the right to possess and occupy it for life, rent-free and without charge except for taxes, insurance, maintenance and related costs and expenses. This right is intended to give the grantor a beneficial interest in the property and to ensure that the grantor does not lose eligibility for a state homestead tax exemption for which she otherwise qualifies.

Part 14. Severability of Clauses

If any provision of this Declaration of Trust is ruled unenforceable, the remaining provisions shall stay in effect.

Certification of Grantor

I certify that I have read this Declaration of Trust and that it correctly states the terms and conditions under which the trust property is to be held, managed and disposed of by the trustee, and I approve the Declaration of Trust.

_____ Dated: _____
John MakerTrust, Grantor and Trustee

CERTIFICATE OF ACKNOWLEDGMENT OF NOTARY PUBLIC
State of _____)
County of _____)

On _____, _____ before me, _____, a notary public in and for said state, personally appeared _____, personally known to me (or proved on the basis of satisfactory evidence) to be the person whose name is subscribed to the within instrument, and acknowledged to me that she/he executed the same in her/his authorized capacity, and that by her/his signature on the instrument the person, or the entity upon behalf of which the person acted, executed the instrument.

Witness my hand and official seal

Notary Public for the State of _____
My commission expires on: _____

Schedule A
Property Placed in Trust
- 100 shares of General Electric Common stock.
- House at 3909 First Street, Los Angeles, Ca.

Printed in the United States
By Bookmasters